A Navigational Guide Toward
Hope and Healing
In the Wake of Addiction

BOUND BY LOVE
ANCHORED IN TRUTH

Desiree Arney CFRS

Sweethaven, New Jersey

Unless otherwise indicated, all Scripture quotations are taken from the Holy Bible, New Living Translation, copyright © 1996, 2005. Used by permission of Tyndale House Publishers, Inc., Wheaton, IL 60189 USA. All rights reserved. Verses marked NIV are taken from the HOLY BIBLE, NEW INTERNATIONAL VERSION®. NIV ®. Copyright © 1973, 1978, 1984 by the International Bible Society. Used by permission of Zondervan. All rights reserved. All emphasis in Scripture quotations has been added by the author.

Note—Advisory
This book is not intended to take the place of sound professional advice, medical or otherwise. Neither the author nor the publisher assumes any liability for possible adverse consequences as a result of the information contained herein. Readers are advised to consult with their physician or other professional practitioners before implementing any suggestions that follow.

While the author has made every effort to provide accurate Internet addresses at the time of publication, neither the publisher nor the author assumes any responsibility for errors, or for changes that occur after release. Further, the publisher does not have any control over and does not assume any responsibility for author or third-party websites or their content.

BOUND BY LOVE— ANCHORED IN TRUTH
A Navigational Guide for Families in the Wake of Addiction
Copyright© 2018 by Desiree Arney
Published by Hearken Books
Sweethaven, NJ 08210

ISBN: 978-1-79709-111-2

All rights reserved. No part of this publication may be reproduced, stored in a retrieval system, or transmitted in any form or by any means—electronic, mechanical, digital, photocopy, recording, or any other—except for brief quotations in printed reviews, without the prior permission of the author. A request form can be found at desireearney.com

DesireeArney.com

Bound By Love—Anchored In Truth

For Lyn & Patrick
BOZ 4-EVER

He will wipe every tear from our eyes, and there will be no more death or sorrow or crying or pain. All these things are gone forever.

Rev 21:4

ACKNOWLEDGMENTS

Thank you to my parents Steve Schulz Sr and Mary for all you did to raise our close family. You are so incredibly missed. God... I can't wait to hug you both! To my brother Steve Jr, sister Val and our sweet lil Cher who have never doubted me, Thank you —

I love you, Jim, for always believing I could do this and for telling me to trust myself and "just write." You have supported every idea and dream in my heart. It means everything. Thanks, Patches, apart from my parents you have been the greatest teacher in my life. When you entered this world, I didn't even know that I had so much to learn about love, life, and sacrifice. Most importantly because of you I learned what truly matters in life–people. Oh, I should probably thank Mike Carmody for making that possible...Thanks, Mike. I am so very grateful for my amazing daughters Taylor and Dayna, you are both so amazingly talented.— Use your gifts to bless others, that's why God gives gifts! Always remember Who's you are. You cannot be anything you want, you cannot do anything you want–But you CAN be who God created you to be and you CAN do anything God calls you to do. Never forget— There is only one you.

To my Soul Sisters, Lyn McCarty, Heidi Hartman, Kelly Gonzalez, Barb Zarrillo, Michele Morris, Vanessa Senni, and Diana Champion, without your love, support, input, and honesty so much would be missing from these pages AND my life! Thank you for being the very best friends in all the land! I appreciate all you have done for me and my family!

I could never forget my mentors, thank you, Dr. Warren and Sandy Saul... what can I say? You know. "Never would have made it through—

if not for God sending you." You are the best, I love you. Thank you to my tribe-The Igniting Souls Team. Kary Oberbrunner my loyal friend and coach. For encouraging me to persevere when I was weak, for challenging me when I held back, and for being at the finish line cheering for me.—Thank you. Paul Zazzo and Samantha Zazzo thank you for coming to our town and teaching my family the true meaning of grace. In my darkest days, you shined His light so that I could see to face another day. I love you both so much.

Kim Maddocks, for nearly 30 years you have spoken truth into my life. Your faithful friendship is a gift I will always cherish. You have taught me about Jesus and living Him out before me. God has used you powerfully to shape my heart toward Him. I love you friend.

I also want to thank the brave and beautiful souls who have shared their broken hearts with me. Your willingness to share your story has fueled this book. Your experience could literally save a life.

Thank you from the bottom of my heart to George and Linda Pharo and the beautiful ladies at Beacon of Hope Bucks Co. So many times your help has made all the difference for those in early recovery. Your generosity has allowed so many to be successful in long term sobriety.

> **Yous Guys:** a northeast phrase meaning you guys. The extra 's' is not silent and is added for no reason whatsoever
>
> –Urban Dictionary

My extended family, Biker family, and friends, you have always come through for our family–we call– you join forces and make things happen. I love you all– Yous Guys are awesome!

I also want to thank the exceptional people working to save lives every day in Bucks County and beyond. It is my privilege and honor to work with you all to help suffering families. I would like to thank Robert Whitley and the Faith In Action Collation of Bucks County PA., Diane Rosati and her caring staff at The Bucks County Drug and Alcohol Commission. Thank you Jay Kurko, Lloyd Gestoso, Andrea Bernek and the entire Bucks County Addiction Task Force for your relentless passion for helping families impacted by Substance Use Disorder.

To my fellow pioneers and very first graduates of the Pennsylvania Certification Board, Certified Family Recovery Specialist at Penn State Abington program. I am so honored to know you and serve with you. I have learned so much from each of you— Aretha Swift, Shannon Kilner, Lisa Dalantinow, Michelle Simmons (Rev), Shane Petry, George Yaeger and Dennis Hallion. We come from different places, but our hearts are the same. I look forward to working with you all to bring hope and healing to suffering families impacted by addiction. A very special thank you to Theresa Bloom, for your part in bringing us together, your dedication and commitment to prepare us reveal your sweet—kind and compassionate heart for those suffering from Substance Use Disorder. To our instructors: James Nestor, MAS, CEAP, LCADC, Stacey Conway, Ph.D, Davin P. Rowe, MS, MA, CAADC, Dana Cohen, MA, M.Ed, and Edythe Cohen, LPC, CCDP and Special Guest Speakers: William F. Brennan, Jr., Philadelphia Police Department (retired) Member, Philadelphia LU#158; Training Specialist; and Renee Cunningham, MSS, Executive Director of Center in the Park, Philadelphia— Thank you sharing your wisdom and experience to equip us to serve in the capacity of supporting fragile family relationships in crisis.

And Above All

My God and Savior Jesus Christ—My Anchor

THANK YOU

You rule the raging of the sea; when the waves arise, You still them.

Psalms 89:9

CONTENTS

Foreword	xi
Purpose	xiii
Introduction	xv

Prepare to Set Sail — 1

Lost At Sea	3
Sinking Our Own Ship	11
Deciding to Change Course	25
Full Steam Ahead	36
Where is God in the Storm?	54
Lifesavers, Loose Cannons, and Castaways	64
Rescue Drowning Mates	72

Never Give Up the Ship! — 80

All Hands on Deck	81
Decide— Course Change	86
Do–Follow The Map	89
Tackle Box	154
Private Quarters	157
Captains Orders	162

FOREWORD

Desiree Arney is a warrior.

There's no other way to put it. She will not back down, shut up, or fade out. She's courageous. She fights for truth and she'll fight for you. She cares for you, your situation, and your pain...because she knows it too well.

It's been said that compassion is your hurt in my heart. Simply put, Desiree has a big heart. I met her many years ago when we joined forces to help people discover freedom from the lies and labels the world throws our way. She supported me, a man with a dream, and for that, I'm forever grateful.

God used a book to bring us together. She found mine, *Your Secret Name*, at a bookstore in New York. She emailed me, and then I called her back. Fast-forward a few months and I met her beautiful family at one of our Your Secret Name events. She was our first team member and with her help, we've ignited over one million souls.

Now Desiree has her own book. She never stopped her passion for changing lives and setting hearts free.

As you read *Bound by Love Anchored in Truth*, you'll see this unique blend of courage and compassion. She won't hold back because she's on a mission. Rather than cursing the darkness, she's lit a candle instead. This book is that light.

Get ready for a transformational journey with a guide who's walked the path. Hold on tight and remember that you have nothing to fear.

The truth will set you free.

– Kary Oberbrunner, author of *Your Secret Name and Elixir Project*

PURPOSE

This book is to help families come together to support, strengthen, and encourage each other when a loved one is in active addiction or working recovery. Addiction affects everyone in the family differently. Many families are simply unequipped to navigate its uncharted waters, and the result can be devastating. Countless families have been torn apart, as each member can respond very differently to the family crisis. Fear of the unknown can cause individuals to react in ways that put more holes in an already sinking ship. We can hardly breathe sometimes under the crashing waves of sorrow and anger. We second-guess and berate ourselves when we make a mistake. We continuously ask what we could or should have done differently. There is a constant battle in our minds that fights to drag our weary souls into the deep.

You and your family will need a compass to travel this difficult journey together. Of course, there are murky and sometimes polluted waters in every family, and not all members will agree at all times. However, if everyone can agree that their loved one is worth fighting for, I think that's a good place to start. This guide can be used by individuals, families, or in a group setting. In whatever way it is used, it is essential to enlist shipmates who will provide a safe haven of support and encouragement along the way. A safe haven can consist of family, friends, group members, or counselors. With the help of this guide, it is possible to demonstrate love by setting healthy boundaries. It is not what is considered today as a Tough Love approach but rather a method to help express love during tough times. My prayer is that the material in this book will help bring some order to your household, a sense of unity to your family, and hope to your heart.

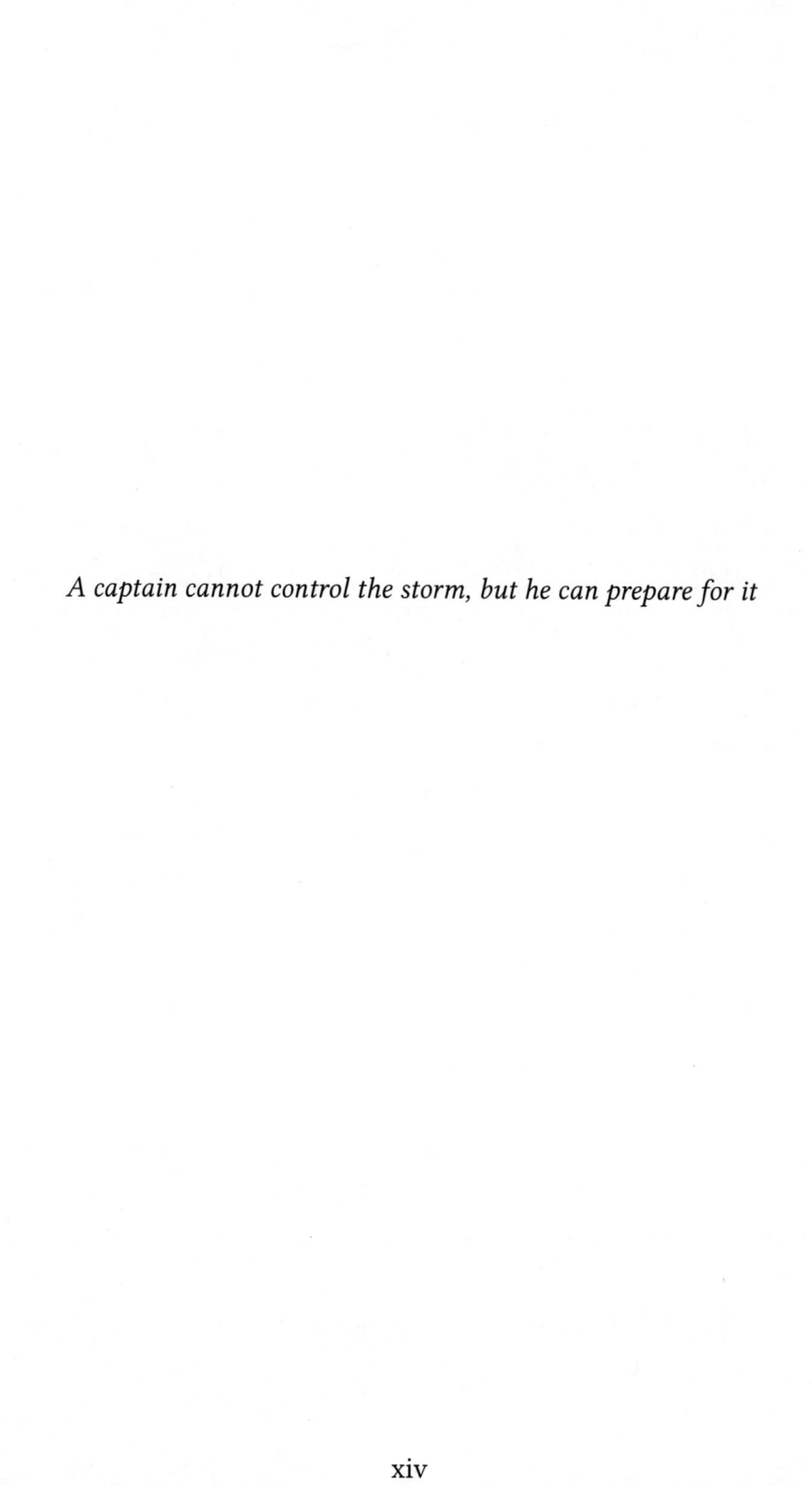

A captain cannot control the storm, but he can prepare for it

INTRODUCTION

Compass: an instrument used for navigation and orientation that shows a direction

The compass we will use in this Voyage is simple:

Determine–Decide–Do

Determine: What is not helping
Decide: What will help
Do: Follow the map

HOW TO USE THIS GUIDE

Part 1 of this book consists of personal accounts, stories others have given me permission to share, and practical examples of how to map your journey. *Bound by Love— Anchored in Truth* is written to get you sailing as quickly as possible, so it is not lengthy or complicated on purpose. I highly recommend reading Part 1 before mapping your Navigation Route. Doing so will help you to understand the overall structure of the Navigation Mapping Process. It will also help clarify what to include in your Navigation Plan that will foster smooth sailing.

Part 2 contains all of the necessary templates to map your family Navigation Route. Your Tackle Box, which, will be a great comfort and help when facing difficult decisions. It includes a prayer guide and scripture to anchor your soul on the journey, no matter what the conditions. God's Word is your life vest. Lastly, you will find helpful resources and links to assist you on your voyage.

PART I

PREPARE TO SET SAIL

ONE

Lost At Sea

She had a home daycare, literally raised nearly every child living in our neighborhood. My best friend Lyn and I spent 15 years raising our mischievous sons together. In those days, her backyard was filled with little ones, snotty noses, dragging swim diapers and infectious toddler belly giggles. Together, we organized games, refereed arguments, and bandaged many boo-boos. We held VBS for the kids every summer and organized fundraisers with them to help those in need at Christmas time. Chaotic as it was back then, somehow Lyn and I kept each other sane in the mayhem of it all. Our sons Patrick and Taylor were best friends the minute they met. Together they took great joy in taunting their little sisters and pulling neighborhood pranks. Both were relentless skateboarders and played video games like it was their job. The two of them were hilariously funny and constantly had us laughing with stories of lunchroom antics. Like all responsible moms, we tried to appear disapproving as they shared details of mission accomplished schemes and practical jokes. However, secretly we were amused by their mischievous boyhood pastimes, as our expressions and unconfined laughter always betrayed us.

The teen years were challenging and, at some point, partying took a dangerous turn. Our sons had to part ways. Although my son had his struggles, her son got swallowed up in our nations heroin addiction tsunami. The years of watching her son spiral downward were heartbreaking and terrifying at the same time. Sleepless nights, gut-wrenching prayers, and relapse after relapse stole her peace and weakened her resolve. The suffocating emotional pain of watching her son drown in addiction seemed to be stealing her very soul.

We had just returned from lunch, Lyn's daycare aid was serving snacks to the kids in the back yard. Lyn's cell phone rang, I stood in her kitchen as she took a call. Earlier at lunch, she had received a few concerning text messages from Taylor, and as she stepped out front, my gut told me something terrible was happening. I walked toward her and stopped suspended in the middle of her hallway, as if between two worlds— a kind of human shield between a nightmare and a daycare. I stood there watching her through the screen door, and it happened all at once. As if in slow motion, the phone dropped from her weak hand and she slumped over on the stairs. I ran out, tried to set her up — yelling, "What's wrong? What happened ?" I grabbed the phone and demanded, "Who is this? What happened?" The voice of Taylor's father said, "Taylor is gone. He overdosed, he's gone." Dropping the phone in shock and horror, I turned to see a few daycare kids coming down the hallway toward us. In desperation, I whispered in her ear, "Please Lyn, please, " I begged. "Let me help you to the stairs to your room and then I will get Bill." She crawled weakly up the stairs sobbing. I got one of the older kids to call parents to come to get their children, then immediately dialed her husband. All I could say was, "It's Taylor," and he knew. I ran up the stairs into Lyn's bedroom to find her in a fetal position on the floor. All I could hear was a deep agonizing moan. She was trembling, sobbing, and screaming all at once, it seemed. It was, so soul-shaking I felt frozen in the terror of the moment. I fell to the ground with her and just held and rocked her until Bill entered the room. For two years, I watched my life filled friend become a shell of a person. So broken, so disillusioned, she appeared to have shut down to all feeling. She simply functioned. Day after day, the reality of her son's death took a piece of her until all I could see in her eyes was —*nothing*.

★ ★ ★

My son has not been the same since he lost Taylor. The bond of brotherhood between them was iron strong, and the loss of that relationship changed my son. It hurt him on a level unreachable by man for healing, but by God, if Pat will allow it. In a real sense my son and I both lost our best friends to addiction that day.

In many ways, I feel I am a forerunner to my friend. I am doing what she will do when she is strong enough to let God redeem her pain to help others. Until she can join me, I will do whatever I can to help fight this enemy. She is slowly emerging from the deep. In a secret way, God is doing a healing work in her. I can see the bright light that once twinkled in her eye make short guest appearances. From a painful sacred place, it flickers and fights to shine. Although mingled with pain, I see hope's light slowly reaching the surface. During these rare moments, I swear I can see the twinkle of Taylor's smile shining through her eyes. The mightiest warriors rise from the worst battles. As she continues to heal and gain strength for combat, one day I know God will raise her up, and I pity the fool who gets in her way. So, for now, I fight, for now, I write, seeking to help families navigate the most difficult places in this painful family crisis. I look forward to the day when she will join me to help strengthen family's impacted by addiction. Every week I have the honor of being part of a network of amazing people who help families battling addiction. We connect families to resources, find placement in treatment centers for their addicted loved ones, and provide them with ongoing support. In many ways, being part of this fight is how I love my friend through her pain. Helping others is an example of what I hope will encourage my son to allow God to use his pain for good. I believe God never wastes our pain, but instead redeems it as we help others to heal. Taylor's story is not over. It's a curious thing that even though Taylor lost his battle, he is saving the lives of so many others—through us.

In the Old Testament, when Nehemiah observed that his comrades were growing weary and distraught because of the deadly threats of the enemy, he reminded them what was at stake. He strengthened his resolve and implored them to stand firm:

> *When I saw their fear, I stood and said to the nobles and officials and the rest of the people: "Do not be afraid of the enemy; [confidently] remember the Lord who is great and awesome, and [with courage from Him] fight for your brothers, your sons, your daughters, your wives, and for your homes."*
>
> *Nehemiah 4:14*

Capsized

Sinking Ship: an impending debacle; an ongoing disaster

Bob ran a very successful construction company. He and his wife Jenny married young and built a life together. While raising five children, they managed to keep their marriage a priority. Together they were determined to teach their children the importance of having a close family with good morals. Despite the time and energy it took to build a business from the ground up, they made time to attend the children's sports and activities regularly. Sometimes they had to split up, one parent going to a football game, while the other sat on the sideline at a soccer tournament. They were present and engaged parents. When Bob discovered that his 19-year-old was involved in drug use, he was destroyed inside. He could not grasp how his son, who was positioned for success in every area of his life, could end up on drugs. Bob's initial shock and anger shifted into feelings of disappointment and fear. He and Jenny launched into action to help him. They sought advice from respected people in the field and found an addiction therapist for their son. They made sure he had access to every available resource. The problem was that their son did not want help. Unlike his parents, who suspected their son was headed for disaster; Jake assured them that he was fine. Jake told them he liked to party and to him he was just a typical college freshman, having a good time. He argued that they were overreacting. Wanting to believe Jake, fostered their denial. Bob and Jenny rationalized that perhaps they were a little over the top. However, quickly the tides turned, and things got out of control. Pot smoking and acid trips led to pill popping, and eventually, intravenous drug use. Jake no longer had a choice.

He craved heroin like a fish out of water. Jake's parents were in a full-blown hurricane with no relief in sight. Daily arguments, ignited by opposing beliefs about how to help their son, ripped at the fabric of their once solid marriage. Constant stress left their entire family tattered and torn.

Weary Shipmates

Addiction tears families apart every day. It is true Substance Use Disorder is a family disease; it impacts everyone. A person in active addiction creates drama, chaos, and confusion at every turn. His behavior causes turmoil within the family regularly. Spouses feel resentment toward each other and siblings have contempt for the brother or sister in addiction. We can begin to heal the strained relationships within our family by first taking responsibility ourselves. We need to apologize if we have allowed a person in addiction to consume us. We should say we are sorry for not being fully present in times when other loved ones have needed us. We can ask for forgiveness for any harm we have caused, however unintentional. We can ask for the opportunity to do better, once we know better. For parents, our other children may not be so quick to forgive or to begin anew. We need to be patient with them; their pain is real. When they consistently observe the positive changes we are making, they may open up. Slowly they might come to appreciate that we are making real efforts to change the family dynamic. We need to demonstrate that we value them as much as we do the sibling that is suffering from Substance Use Disorder. We cannot just assume that they know we appreciate them. They have to experience it consistently, in our actions. A broken family can rebuild damaged relationships–sometimes making them even stronger than before.

Deep Waters, Slowly Drowning

> **Uncharted Waters:** Territory unknown or explored. Entering conditions without navigation skills

Tears welled in her eyes as she drifted back in her memory to tell me about her daughter who lives in the streets of Philadelphia. "I can't sleep, I can't eat, my marriage is in trouble, my boss is running out of patience with me," she sighed. Her beautiful, smart, "A" student, 20-year-old daughter had a full ride scholarship to university. She was now selling her body to feed her veins. "My daughter had everything going for her Des, then she met this guy." She went on to share that her daughter had ADHD, was bullied as a preteen, and that at two years old, her father left them. I first met Mandy when she walked into a support group that I was leading for families impacted by addiction. She appeared to be rumbling inside, like a volcano ready to erupt. She worked hard to keep her composure as she sat quietly listening to others in the group. Her head nodded in agreement and communicated assurance that she had an intimate understanding of what was being said. She shook her head with indignant disbelief as a dad tearfully shared a heartbreaking story. A mom shared about the horrible treatment her son experienced by hospital staff following an overdose, that was successfully reversed. The rage communicated through her body language was evident as another parent told of a treatment center where her son bought heroin from the night shift cleaning staff. I have experienced her outrage. A combination of terror, anger, and sorrow threaten to drown any hope for better days.

> **Landlubber:** an unseasoned sailor or someone unfamiliar with the sea

True stories like this are shared by millions of families. If you are reading this book, chances are you are desperate to find a new or different approach to help a person you love. You long to bring some form of peace back into your home.

We are landlubbers, sailing uncharted waters without sea legs. No wonder we are sinking! Most of us who find ourselves aboard this ship have no sailing experience. We are uncertain about how to help a person in active addiction, or how to support their recovery. So we do the best we know until we know better. Sometimes, we have to take a different approach. It is always best to plan rather than react. To begin with, it is essential to clearly identify what is not helping your addicted loved one. Doing so will give you clarity to decide on other ways you can provide support.

Let's clear some of the fog to see where we are...

TWO

Sinking Our Own Ship

Excuses might even be found for a thief if he steals when he is starving! But even so, he is fined seven times as much as he stole, though it may mean selling everything in his house to pay it back

Proverbs 6:30-31 NIV

Many parents I meet are living in a fog. They cannot see that they may be unintentionally putting more holes in an already sinking ship. What I saw in Mandy as she talked with me about her daughter was— myself. I don't think we are alone either, many of us do this, whether our child is using drugs or not. We defend and make excuses for our child's poor choices. We instinctively protect our children by any means necessary. Even when harmful things happen to them through no fault of their own, we will use the misfortune to rationalize their poor choices. My son was driving home one afternoon and was hit by an intoxicated driver. The young man was speeding in a dump truck and plowed into my son at 45 mph. He was seriously injured and suffers to this day as a result. Watching him struggle with the physical, emotional, and spiritual implications of the accident were incredibly difficult for me. As a result, I made many excuses to myself and others when my son made irresponsible choices. Most of the things I did to help him, he never even asked me to do. I blamed outside influences to answer the question that baffles idealistic parents like me: "Why in the world would my smart, caring, madly handsome, incredibly talented son, make a bad decision?". That's not very realistic, I know. What is true is that his pain was, and is real, his injuries great, his suffering an injustice, but I let those things define him. My perception was narrow; I saw him as a victim of the world around him, which determined the kind of help I provided. Looking back, what I believed he needed was not always what was best. Some of my well-meaning help voided opportunities for him to learn. He was, in fact, a victim, but he was also a survivor. My empathy for his suffering fogged my vision to see his strengths. He deserved compassion for his suffering and understanding for what happened to him, but he also needed encouragement and support to rise above adversity. Reflecting back I also realize that many of the things he did or did not do, were simply because he was a typical teenager or college freshman. Sometimes he didn't get things done, because he procrastinated. Sometimes his lack of focus was because he was not committed to staying focused. Not everything was due to injuries from the accident. Do you see? Not every failure, flaw, or set back is to blame for why our kids are riotous, irresponsible, or reckless.

Even if there is a place for blame, it does not exempt anyone from the negative or harsh consequences of poor choices. In his no-nonsense series, *Total Transformation*, James Lehman is blunt:

> Your child may have ADHD, Bipolar, Depression, an absent parent, significant loss, no friends. Doesn't matter. The law doesn't care. A person may act out and do wrong things because of certain life events, but ultimately a judge must make his ruling

based on the law. He must rule justly based on crimes committed not the reasons why.

A person is accountable regardless of what they have suffered or the negative situations they have encountered. It is our responsibility to help our children learn from their mistakes. And if we just get out of the way, natural consequences will be the most effective teacher. If anyone had a good reason to make bad choices, it was James. Born in 1946, he was abandoned in the basement of an apartment building at only 18 months old. Mr. Teddy Lehman found him, and he and his wife went on to adopt James. Although James was rescued and provided a stable home, there were no guarantees. Childhood abandonment wounds perfectly positioned James for a future of drug use and crime. He states,

> I dropped out of high school at a young age and got into trouble with alcohol, drugs and the police. I wound up doing a significant amount of time in prisons and institutions during my teen and young adult years. I didn't know how to deal with the obstacles life presented, so I turned to drugs and alcohol. Crime gave me access to and the means to buy both. From the age of 17 to 20 I was in prison, and that's where I got my high school diploma. In my early adulthood, I hitchhiked across the country twice; I was trying to leave behind the life I'd created for myself. But no matter where I went, I couldn't get away from drugs and alcohol, which always brought me back to criminal behavior–which in turn, brought me back to jail. It was a dangerous, negative cycle I couldn't seem to escape from on my own.

It wasn't until James was ordered by a judge to a treatment center, that he was offered hope. The clinical approach primarily targeted and confronted poor behavior and self-destructive patterns. The focus was not so much on the emotional, physical, and psychological damage he experienced, although they were factors in his overall treatment plan. James participated in therapy sessions designed to examine and determine how his poor choices were hurting him further. The therapeutic approach included exercises to help participants identify self-absorbed and faulty thinking patterns. James learned, that although he could not change what happened to him, he had the power to change the way it affected him. To remedy victim mentalities, clinicians introduced the idea of helping others and giving back as a new method of function. James gained a new perspective on life. He went on to become one of the most effective and well-respected counselors in the country–helping thousands of struggling families.

We are not truly helping when we rescue someone from experiencing the consequences of poor choices. We have to change the way we think about this. We have to ask ourselves different questions that bring a new perspective, such as "Will the help I offer, position a person to make responsible choices in the future?" We have to examine our motives. Many times we give in to requests, not because we believe it will help someone, but to avoid the guilt we will feel if we don't. In other words, the help we give is more about soothing our conscience. A couple I know dared to take a closer look at their motives for helping their daughter. The couples' daughter would continuously ask for money to pay her rent, get diapers, and fix her car. Based on clear evidence, their daughter did not spend the money they gave her on anything she claimed to need. This was obvious when they paid her a visit. Her car still had a flat, there was little food in the pantry, and her baby had terrible diaper rash. During the visit, eviction warning notices cluttered her kitchen table. On top of them was the most recent, a bright orange Final Eviction Notice. She demonstrated all the signs of using drugs, but her parents kept financing her irresponsibly. Why? When exploring their actions deeper to understand their thinking, they discovered that guilt and fear dictated their decisions. The underlying motivation was that they could not live with the guilt of allowing their daughter to be hungry or homeless. Even though the facts indicated that the things they feared were bound to happen anyway, it eased their conscience to keep giving. They have since changed their approach.

As parents or guardians, we have a responsibility to teach and demonstrate God's love. Even the Father in heaven allows His children to experience the natural consequences of sin. We should do no less. This is especially true when our children are growing up because consequences make provision for personal growth. Experiencing the pain associated with a bad decision cultivates wisdom. Pain also provides fertile soil to develop character and grow faith, and when we rescue, we interfere with God's best for them. The author of Hebrews reminded fellow believers:

> *"Being punished isn't enjoyable while it is happening–it hurts! But afterward, we can see the result, a quiet growth in grace and character"*
>
> *Hebrews 12:11*

Storm Warning

It is also vital to prepare our children to be aware of pitfalls and potential dangers. Before his passing, the Apostle Paul warned his comrades that the days ahead would be hard. Paul told them that wolves would come attempting to lead them astray to shipwreck their faith. "Hope in Christ," he said. He told them this to prepare them to stand firm when facing difficulty and hardship. We have an enemy who comes in many forms; sometimes disguised as an angel of light to deceive us. Our lives require connection and sensitivity to God's voice to direct us at all times. Bad things happen, but God promises that He is close to the brokenhearted. Faith in God develops through adversity, and rescuing our children at every turn interferes with that process. It also hinders their ability to develop critical life skills. We have to instill in our children that life hurts sometimes, but God is with us. Faith is being sure of what we believe, even if it doesn't feel like it or look like it. My point is, we need to be purposeful and prayerful when we provide or offer to help. If we block natural consequences and soften discipline, we teach our kids a terrible lie–the Lie of Entitlement. Our children expect us to provide immediate relief every time they feel discomfort because it is what we have taught them. The world at large cares little about what our child has been through; it's ruthless. We do need to protect them to some degree, but we also have to allow them to learn to survive in the real world. Life is unfair, and the sooner young people understand that, the better. Remember, as long as you are a parent, it's never too late to begin teaching this. Setting new boundaries may be uncomfortable in the short term, but it is best for everyone in the long run. It is never too late to take back your parental position. Now is the time to determine what you will and will not allow in your life. Now is the time to stop taking responsibility for your child's behavior and actions. Whether your child is young or old, the time is now.

The same goes for marital relationships. If we allow our spouse to continue behaviors that negatively impact our children, like exposure to drug use or domestic violence, it is abuse. If we do not take action in situations like this, we become a party to the abuse. Calling our husband's job to tell them he is sick, when in truth he has a massive hangover, is not being a supportive wife. We may do this because we are afraid our husband will lose his job. In reality, the entire family is already suffering because of his reckless and irresponsible behavior–not to mention the fact that, if not treated, alcoholism progresses. Things will continue to get worse. Our decision to cover for him may spare his job for a while, but it won't motivate changed behavior. However, if we refuse to take responsibility for his actions, the natural consequence of losing his job just might. In her incredibly insightful book, *The Emotionally Destructive Marriage: How to Find Your Voice and Reclaim Your Hope,* Leslie Vernick says that when we excuse our husbands' poor choices and bad behavior, we are actually helping them to sin against God.

> Right about now you realize that you have some difficult choices in front of you. Believe me, I know change is hard, and sometimes we're only motivated to change when the pain of staying the same becomes greater than the fear or pain of making the change. You can choose to grow stronger through this destructive marriage or not, but if you choose to do nothing, you need to understand what it will cost you: your emotional, mental, and spiritual core will get weaker and weaker, curving inward until your entire personhood is out of alignment. Sacrificing yourself by allowing someone to sin against you to keep peace in your marriage is never a wise choice–not for you, not for your husband, not for your marriage.

It is never easy to confront or navigate conflict, but the longer we delay, the more damage being done to the entire family. Dr. Phil says, "What we allow– will continue." These are wise words that have been pivotal in helping me decide what I will and will not allow in my life.

Sharon found herself in a constant state of simmering anger. The knot in her stomach and gnawing ache in her heart never seemed to let her breathe an untroubled breath. She had not had a peaceful night's sleep in three years. Regularly, She made stops at the local courthouse to pay her adult daughter's fines. When she wasn't doing that, she was looking into classes she thought her daughter should take. She found herself doing many things because she desperately wanted her to turn her life around. Sharon bought her daughter stuff she could not afford because she felt sorry for her. She filled out job applications and even set up interviews with potential employers! Her life was consumed with "helping" her daughter. Sharon's controlling nature rarely got the result she hoped for, and in fact, produced many bad arguments with her daughter. Sharon had the misguided belief that if she could fill her life with positive things, she would not relapse. Worse, she believed that if her daughter did relapse, it would be her fault for not doing enough. Daily, her mind swirled with a million dreaded thoughts. She was emotionally, mentally, and physically drained but could not rest; fear ruled her day and worry robbed her nights.

We need to recognize that people have free will. What we do to "help" someone could result in a positive outcome, but is never guaranteed. For example, we can choose to pay for college for our son, but that doesn't ensure that he will finish well. We can get our boss to give our daughter a job, but that doesn't mean she will show up for work. We can try to control everything and everyone around us, but this will never guarantee anything. One mom I know would push aside other important responsibilities to help her son. She would cancel plans with family and friends to accommodate his schedule. Every time her son needed a ride somewhere, she would drop everything and take him. Her other relationships began to suffer, and family members started to harbor resentment toward the two of them. In this instance, her son was only four months sober, and she feared he would relapse if she didn't make sure he was safe from temptations to use. Her thought was that if she didn't take him where he wanted to go, he would call someone who could possibly take him to get drugs. Her heart would not let her take that chance. In her mind, she believed she was helping her son. In reality, she was communicating that she did not trust him and she interfered with his ability to trust himself. Her help was hurting him. Meanwhile, she neglected responsibilities and damaged other important relationships. Of course, that was not her intention, but whenever actions are dictated by fear, it is almost impossible to see anything else. It is critical to examine how we think because thoughts dictate actions.

In the above situation, my friend thought about a possible bad outcome but operated as if it was fact. Her thoughts of what might happen ignited fears that overpowered logic, which motivated her actions. This is the vicious and relentless thought process that keeps us blind to logical and wise decisions. We have to ask God to give us the courage to face ourselves and challenge our motives for why we do what we do. Obviously, my friend wanted to help her son remain sober, but placing him under a microscope revealed a desperate attempt to save them both. Her inner voice said, "I cannot bury my son." These thoughts terrified and tormented her daily. Stripped down, the things she did to help her son were desperate attempts to control the future. But we have to face the fact that no matter what we do to avoid our worst fear, it could still happen. This is the reason I am so passionate about reminding people that faith in God is not believing Him for a specific outcome. It is trusting Him to be with us no matter what the outcome.

In her empowering book, *Setting Boundaries with Your Adult Child,* Allison Bottke helps readers rest assured that they are not responsible for the choices of their adult children. She reminds burdened parents to stop owning what doesn't belong to them:

> Because it's not our fault if our adult child didn't wake up in the morning to get to his job and he gets fired and therefore doesn't get paid and therefore can't pay his child-support and therefore gets arrested. It's not our fault if he doesn't have clean clothes to wear for his job interview or enough gas in his car to get to work. It's not our fault if his cell phone gets shut off for

nonpayment and he gets evicted for not paying his rent. It's not our fault if he fails another class because he didn't stay home and do his homework and instead went out to party. It's not our fault if he says yes to a drug pusher who hands him a dirty needle or if he gets behind the wheel while drunk and ends up killing an innocent bystander. It's not our fault if he gets caught up in illegal activity that lands him behind bars, and it's not our fault if he sees suicide as his only way out of the bondage that is holding him prisoner.

We have to learn to stop making ourselves sick with worry. We cannot live in a world of "what if's". We only have the power to control our own actions. We have to stop living as if the whole world will fall apart if we don't manage every problem our family members create. We have to stop cleaning up messes that we did not make. It's that simple, but not that easy.

Assessing Conditions:

A good way to determine whether the things we do help or hurt the situation, is to ask ourselves honest questions. It is the first step toward healing our family and helping an addicted loved one.

Honest answers to the questions below will do two things:

1. Shed light on what is driving us when we help.

2. Uncover the behaviors that we need to change.

Specifically, we need to ask ourselves:

Honest Question:

Why do I give money to my daughter for rent even though I suspect she is probably not using it to pay her rent?

Honest Answer:

Because if I don't, she will lose her apartment. If she loses her apartment, she will be homeless. I cannot live with myself if anything bad happens to her on the streets. Plus, I don't want to believe that she is lying to me; it's too painful.

The following questions will help identify the things we need to change:

1. What do I find myself doing for an addicted loved one that causes me to feel angry while I am doing it?

2. What ways have I tried to help my loved one that leaves me wondering or doubting my decision?

3. What do I spend time doing for an addicted loved one that is stealing time from other important relationships?

4. What do I provide or allow that contributes to my addicted loved ones ability to remain irresponsible?

5. What do I do for my addicted loved one that she can and should be doing for herself?

Do you do any of the following?

- Lie to others to cover up someone's poor choices or irresponsible behavior?

- Make appointments, pay bills, run errands (basically, take the role of a personal assistant)?

- Pay a cell phone bill, but do not get paid back?

- Allow an able-bodied young person or adult to be unemployed and live at home?

- Give Money?

- Loan things: car, money, even if it inconveniences you?

- Pay fines?

- Act like you do not see drug usage that is apparent?

- Pay for college, but presented with failing grades?

- Stop doing something you enjoy so you can handle a matter that is not your responsibility or concern?

Some of these questions may cause feelings of guilt, embarrassment, or shame for not addressing mistakes that seem so obvious now. But, again, there is no room for any of that. It's a new day.

There is great freedom that comes from releasing responsibilities that do not belong to us. Since I have started to identify areas where I was stepping in to fix what someone else broke, I have begun to push back. I started practicing the art of pause. A pause is when I take deliberate mental action to attentively assess a situation. During the pause, I ask myself pointed questions that help me make better decisions. These are questions like:

- Who created this situation?
- Why is it happening?
- Who is actually responsible for dealing with it?
- What, if anything, will I do about it?
- Should I be involved?
- What are some possible outcomes, if I do get involved?

We can rely on the past as a guide to make wiser decisions that offer hope for the future. Change is possible. We just need God's help.

THREE

Deciding to Change Course

Don't say anything you don't mean

Matthew 5:33 The Message

One way to determine what we are doing that is not helping our loved one is to decide what will. Something that will change immediately when following this guide is that written agreements will replace idle threats. It's important to be realistic, practical, and honest with ourselves when deciding these things. Words are easy to say, but, as we all know, following through can be difficult. When we are faced with having to act on the threats we have made, fear can consume us. Quickly, we mentally bag up our words and toss them overboard. For example, my friend told her son that if he came home high again, he would be forced to leave and he could never come back. When he did, she told him to go into his room and sleep it off. She then rationalized and excused his behavior: "His girlfriend broke up with him today, that's why he used— because he's so hurt." This was followed by more self-talk to excuse her behavior. She asked herself, justifying her inaction,

"How can I make him leave? How can I reject him, like his girlfriend did?" In the name of compassion, she retracted her boundary based on circumstances, instead of holding him accountable for his wrong actions. When she made the threat, she was clear about what he could expect to happen. Her lack of follow-through communicated to her son that her words were meaningless. She was actually teaching her son that her rules didn't really apply. The most important part of the Navigation Plan is that it include only the consequences we are committed to enforcing. It is wise to carefully think through boundaries before setting them, and what the consequences will be if they are crossed.

Captain Cathy

Cathy decided that when her son got out of treatment, things would be different. Typically, her son would finish an inpatient program and then come back home to live. He was never in a hurry to find a job or to work any ongoing recovery program. Before long, he'd be using again. After his seventh treatment center, she knew she had to change, or nothing else would. While he was still in treatment, she shared her expectations. She told him that she would bring an agreement with her to the next visit. She explained that once he read it, he could decide if he was willing to honor the terms and sign it, or not. She knew he doubted her intentions, but she assured him that she was very serious. The following week she brought the agreement. One of the expectations included in the agreement was that her son work full-time. Among other things, she told him that if he used again, he could not come back home–not even if he went to treatment. Her son agreed to the terms, but not long after, he started missing work. He had no legitimate reason for not going to work. He also would not disclose where he was during those hours. According to the agreement, her son had to leave her home. She told me that following through on her word was one of the most difficult things she had ever done. Three weeks later, he called begging for another chance. She gave him a number for a treatment center and told him she loved him, then hung up. Approximately one month later, he called asking to come home. She gave him a phone number for a halfway house that provides room and board in exchange for work on the farm. He wasn't happy. She continued to show loving support by visiting him often at the farm and encouraging him in his efforts to remain sober. Keeping her word positioned her son to make different choices. It also changed the dynamic of their relationship because he was no longer permitted to control or use her to get what he wanted. Slowly, trust and respect for each other began to grow, and they have a very close relationship today.

> **Mayday:** an international radio distress signal used especially by ships and aircraft, meaning `help me'

A few years ago, Kelly called me in a panic. I have known Kelly since high school. Familiar with my background, she reached out to me for some direction. "I think my daughter is on drugs, Des," she said, in a voice desperately hoping it was not the case. "She's skipping school, she has lost 20 pounds, and she's falling asleep in the middle of conversations." Kelly had reason to be concerned. I had little doubt that her daughter was using so I told Kelly not to delay. "Go get a drug test, and tell her she has to take it," I instructed her to tell her daughter about her suspicions. The test would tell. Kelly was fearful. She implored, "What if she thinks I don't trust her?" I told her that if her daughter is taking drugs, offending her would be the least of her worries. "Get to the truth," I said. When her daughter came home, Kelly told her she had concerns and presented the test. Her daughter denied using drugs and refused to take the test. When Kelly insisted, her daughter became angry and started yelling. It was the beginning of a long battle to save her daughter. Every passing day, Kelly watched her daughter slowly self-destruct. She felt powerless.

One terrifying night her daughter was at a friend's house and overdosed. An ambulance was called, and the EMT was able to revive her with Narcan. That incident sent Kelly begging her daughter's school guidance counselor for help. Finally, she was able to obtain a court order to force her daughter into treatment. It was an emotionally exhausting and gut-wrenching experience for the entire family. The hardest part, she told me, was hearing her daughter spew hateful words at her. It was agonizing. After 16 years of granting wishes, to save her daughters life, Kelly had to deny her wish to forgo treatment. Today Kelly and her daughter are closer than ever. Her daughter is a freshman in college and volunteers at a teen center for at-risk girls.

Earlier this month, I coached a woman struggling to follow through on her word. She told her son several weeks earlier that she would no longer give him money, under any circumstances. Her son called her that morning and kept calling. He was succeeding at breaking her down, so she called me. The son was harassing her relentlessly, demanding that she send him money. He told her that if she sent him money one last time, he would go to treatment. She kept telling him, no, but he continued pressuring her. He went so far as to say that he had a stroke because he was withdrawing. She decided to stop answering his texts, but her silence only fueled his desperation. He knew her weaknesses and targeted his messages accordingly. In a last ditch effort, he even used their close relationship to riddle her with guilt and fear to get what he wanted. The text message read:

> You said you would never give up on me. I'm sorry mom, but I can't keep doing this. Goodbye, mom, you're my world, and I love you, but it ends now.

At my urging, she communicated with him one last time to instruct him not to contact her until he was in a treatment center. She was able to say this with confidence because a day earlier I made arrangements for her son to be picked up by treatment transport. All he had to do was call, and the treatment center would arrange to pick him up. Yet for two more days, he continued to leave offensive, threatening voice messages. He was so used to her giving in, that when she told him the terms for communicating further, he tested her. She passed! It was only then that he finally surrendered and called the treatment center for transportation.

One of the best boundaries I have learned is to delay an answer. I try to never answer a request without thinking it through. This practice has helped me to make much better decisions than I once did. Delaying an answer gives me time to consider the full scope of the question thoughtfully. When someone in recovery asks for help, it is wise to get into the habit of not answering immediately. Try not to agree to anything right away. Be sure you understand what the caller is asking and why. Never commit to anything on the first call or conversation—just listen. Then tell them you will get back to them shortly. Even if they are not used to this response from you, they should respect your decision to think about it. Usually, if they are being truthful and the request is legitimate, they will not object to waiting. I have found that when someone is being dishonest with me, whatever she is requesting, is presented as a dire emergency. Typically, this is a tactic a person will use in the hope that you agree to what she wants without questioning her. It's a good indicator that things are not as they appear— especially if they start yelling at you. In this case, simply say to them something like, "If you cannot let me think about this, and you need an answer right now, then the answer is 'No.'" It is also common for someone in recovery who has relapsed, to offer what I call "word salads." This is when she attempts to answer your questions promptly and confidently, but her answers do not really make sense. This can be tricky because a person practiced in serving "word salad" can sound like she is on the up and up. If you suspect something is not adding up, keep asking questions. Like William Paul Young said, "Our words tell on us." Inevitably, if the person is lying, she will trip up. For example, a family member called one night and said she needed money to get a Vivitrol shot. She knew I would feel it was imperative for her to have the shot. She added an element of urgency by saying she was feeling the temptation to use. She further added that the place she was scheduled to get the shot was only open for a short amount of time. These were all tactics to get me to make a decision immediately. I did not fall for this and gave my usual response, "Let me get back to you in 15 minutes." During that time, I made a few calls and was able to schedule her to receive the Vivitrol shot free of charge. I even offered to take her. She said she would call me back but never did.

It has been very empowering for me to establish a mental list of personal boundaries. God gives me wisdom when I ask, I talk to Him a lot lately. I also use unspoken internal statements to gain perspective. I talk to myself a lot lately. These two practices give me discernment, especially when I suspect someone may be using manipulative tactics to get what they want. For example, I ask "God please,"

1. Give me wisdom to discern the truth about this situation.

2. Give me courage to look at facts of the matter.

3. Give me strength to follow Your lead to navigate through it.

I say to myself, "Now listen here Self,"

1. Just because this person says something, does not make it true.

2. You do not have to do what this person is asking. You always have a choice.

3. The result of this person's careless actions or lack of planning does not automatically become your emergency.

Think about the last few conversations you had that were contentious. What can you remember about each exchange to help determine your thought process during the conversation? Analyzing your internal dialog can change your life. Someone once said, "You gotta think about — what you're thinking about." It is a good way to identify faulty thinking patterns that warrant a change.

Necessary Detours —Steering Conversations

Many families build unhealthy bonds with each other that originate with discovering that a loved one is using drugs. It starts out innocently enough. We rely on each other to process the initial shock and confusion of it all. However, at some point conversations begin to center on the addicted person most of the time. Usually, in the absence of the person struggling in addiction, family members revisit incidents and rehearse wrongs caused or committed by the addicted loved one. Doing this only fuels bitterness and resentment. Anyone can fall into the habit of participating in negative talk that only perpetuates discord and prevents healing for everyone. In my friend Terry's family, this was the case.

Terry was beside herself. Her daughter, Sienna, has been battling addiction for over eight years. One day she called me upset about her other adult daughter, Madison. Madison was mad at her mother because she gave a cell phone to Sienna when she was released from treatment to a recovery house. I asked Terry why her daughter would be angry about that. She told me that Madison was tired of Sienna taking advantage of everyone. After sending a quick prayer to God for wisdom, I made a suggestion. I told her that she might want to consider setting some boundaries for her other adult children– Boundaries like telling them that she does not want to talk about Sienna or discuss her decisions involving her anymore. I went on to say, "We don't answer to our kids, Terry. Your other children do not have to like what you do. That is their choice. But you need to have confidence in your decisions as a mother and stand up for yourself." It is easy for families to form a habit of bad-mouthing or bashing the addicted in conversations. It is a good idea to limit how much and how often details are discussed. Other family members may have opinions about what they think a parent should do, but it is not their decision to make. We should love all of our children the same. However, we may have very different approaches toward each in our parenting. Our other kids may not understand how or why we do what we do when it comes to this, and that's okay. Many siblings of an addict feel pushed aside and like less of a priority to their parents. These frustrations and disappointments often manifest in angry verbal rants about the addicted sibling. A parent can, and should, try to do better at being more available and in tune with the other children. When we are with them or talking with them on the phone, they should be our focus. It is a good idea to change the subject to what is happening in their lives. If they ask about the addicted sibling just say something like, "I don't want to discuss that now. Let's talk about what's new with you." If you recognize this pattern in your family, try to steer conversations in another direction. If you do this enough, the new habit should replace the old. If that doesn't work, you could always tell your family what Tom Carmody tells his: "If you don't have nothin nice to say, shut up." As a catalyst for change in your family, making decisions like redirecting negative conversations or refusing to engage in a rehearsal of wrongs may seem small, but the impact may surprise you.

> *Slander no one, to be peaceable and considerate, and always to be gentle toward everyone.*
>
> *Titus 3:2*

Brave New World

Making an active decision is empowering. Passive decision making is when we simply allow what is happening–to happen. We are still making a decision, a decision not to act. We can place responsibility back where it belongs, on the one attempting to make his problem, ours. It just takes some practice. Start now, with a few staples:

"No, I am not responsible for your feelings."

"No, I can't do that for you."

"No, I am not going to rescue you from the consequences of your own irresponsible behavior."

"No, I am not going to arrange my life around trying to maintain an image of perfection."

No is a complete sentence. ~Ann Lamont

To draw a clear map for your journey, you will have to:

- Decide what you will do.
- Decide what you will no longer do.
- Decide what you will allow.
- Decide what you will no longer allow.
- Decide specific and detailed consequences if agreements are broken.
- Decide who will be your shipmates to support you on this journey.

Of course, it will not be smooth sailing all the time. Life will always present challenging situations. Don't be afraid to make decisions. Decide. And trust God to give you the strength to follow through.

FOUR

Full Steam Ahead

The greatest threat to bringing about lasting change within our family is the lack of follow through on the consequences stated in our Family Navigation Plan. It's a sink or swim situation. We have to mean what we say and say what we mean, **every time.** Until there is consistent long-term compliance to the boundaries that are set, there is no room for adjustments or leniency. We will be tempted to question ourselves as to whether we may have been too hasty in setting the boundary in the first place. We are very capable of doing all kinds of mental gymnastics to avoid our own discomfort when it comes to executing consequences. For this reason, we need to have a steadfast resolve to implement what we have agreed to before any boundary is ever broken. Credibility is paramount if we ever hope to motivate change. Our minds must be set.

A Port of Call: an intermediate stop for a ship on its sailing itinerary

Pre-Sail Preparations

Begin with a casual mention to your struggling loved one of your desire to make some changes in your life. You may mention that you are reading a book that helps families understand addiction. Or that you are discovering things about yourself by reading it. You may add that you are considering the possibility of joining a family support group. Now, be warned the person with Substance Use Disorder will not be happy with your new bold moves toward getting your life back. It will irritate them because it will require more of them, but stand firm! Remember why you are doing this in the first place. It is to identify what is not truly helping them and to decide what to change that will. It is to bring structure to your family and peace within your home. Casual conversation about your plans for upcoming changes will provide the perfect segway to introducing your Navigation Plan to the addicted loved one.

Once your Map is drawn, you can set sail. Begin by explaining that you want to set a time to talk that works for both of you. Be clear about the nature of the sit-down—to go over changes that will impact them. Be prepared to discuss changes you will make and your expectations going forward. It is wise to set up a future time, so the person does not feel attacked. To just spring on someone the statement, "We gotta talk," with no warning, will likely be met with defensiveness.

Let's look at a sample script of a mom who is ready to ship off–
Bon Voyage!

Mary Sets Sail

Setting: Mary is a single mom of an adult daughter, Jillian has been struggling with alcohol addiction and drug abuse for six years. She is 25 years old, has failed out of college, and has little ambition to do anything that requires much of her. Jillian has been in and out of treatment four different times. She is two weeks out of rehab with no plan. Based on past results Mary realizes that many things she has done to help her daughter, have harmed her instead. Mary wants to do things differently this time. She begins by sharing with Jillian that she is looking at recovery in a new light.

Scene 1-

Setting: The kitchen, 7:00 am Mary is about to leave for work. Jillian is sitting on the sofa with a cup of coffee.

Mary: You know Jillian, I've been reading this book, and it's helping me understand how I can better support your recovery. I'll have to tell you about it when we have more time.

Jillian: Ok.

Mary: I have joined a support group as well, and I am learning a lot. I realize that some of the things I have done to help you, are really hurting you. That's the last thing I want.

Jillian: Like what?

Mary: Let's talk about it when I get home.

Scene 2-

Setting: The dinner table later that evening.

Mary: So I was saying earlier that this book I am reading is really eye-opening. Once I finish reading it, I'd like to set a time when we can sit down and discuss some things, OK?

Jillian: Ok– whatever.

Scene 3-

Setting: Saturday morning, a week later at breakfast:

Mary: Jillian, I mentioned that I would like to talk some things over with you.

Jillian: Yeah, what about it?

Mary: I want to set a time that works for both of us, so I can share with you some changes I plan to make to help you.

Jillian: OK, whenever …I guess

Mary: Ok tomorrow after dinner, about 6:30 pm ok?

Jillian: Yeah.

Scene 4-

Setting: The next day 7:30pm at the kitchen table.

Starting the Conversation:

Mary: Jillian I have tried to support your sobriety by offering my help, but as I am learning, I could be helping you fail. In the past when you were in active addiction, I did everything I could to stop your choices from ruining your future. For example, I paid your credit cards so you wouldn't get bad credit. I bailed you out of jail because you promised to change. That did not happen. I gave you money never requiring you to repay me. I allowed you to live here rent-free so you could save money to move out. But you have made no attempts to find a job. I took steps to minimize the negative impact that your own poor choices would have on you, instead of letting you learn from your mistakes. All through your addiction, recovery, and relapse; I have been here for you trying to support your sobriety. After four relapses, obviously what I am doing is not working. This time I am doing things differently. It is time for you to take responsibility for your own life. I want to be open and honest with you. The changes I am making will require you to make changes as well. Transitions are difficult for everyone, but are necessary for growth.

Jillian: Ok...Mom..?

Mary continues, despite Jillian's attempts to make Mary feel small for being naive enough to think a book could enlighten her.

Mary: I have some examples of how my help is hurting you:

By paying your credit cards, I taught you that you did not have to pay for things you have purchased.

Bailing you out of jail taught you that your actions had little consequence.

Giving you money erased your incentive to work.

Making excuses for your poor decisions have allowed you to remain immature and behave irresponsibly.

Doing things for you, that you should have been doing for yourself, communicated my lack of confidence in your abilities.

The type of help I want to offer from now on will provide opportunities for you to step up, make different choices, and take charge of your life.

(*she continues*)

> I want to discuss a structured timeline for transitions that are both realistic and reasonable. Let's work together. I am still here for you as I have always been. My help is just going to look different now. What I am doing is not punishment; it is a new way to support you in recovery. I have made these decisions because I believe they will actually help you succeed in recovery and in life.

Mary has already determined the things she has done that do not help her daughter. Now she will share what she has decided will help.

Mary: A few changes that will change immediately are these:

> I will not give you any more money.
>
> I will not allow you to be unemployed and live here.
>
> I will no longer allow you to live here for free.
>
> I will not rescue you from the consequences of your poor choices.

At this point, Jillian begins to react as she usually does when she feels pressure or is confronted with change. She is rolling her eyes, crossing her arms, and expressing disbelief at the audacity of her mother withholding what she believes is her right. Her voice elevated, Jillian demands that Mary provide solutions for the 'problems' that her mother's plan has created for her future.

Jillian: How am I supposed to get a job if you don't give me money to get an Uber to get there? How can I pay you to live here, if you won't help me with transportation? What kind of job am I going to get with a criminal record? How am I supposed to save money if I have to pay my fines and pay you to stay here?

Mary: Well Jill, we can discuss all of that and figure out the details of how you can accomplish those things. I am not saying that I will not help you at all, but that the help I now offer, will support definite goals. The changes I have decided to make are happening immediately. They are not up for debate. Thinking about how you will accomplish each obstacle you mentioned should be your focus, not making excuses for why it cannot be done.

Jillian: You don't get it. You read some book, and now you're an expert? Yeah, OK. (why, yes Jillian, yes she is...)

Mary: Look, like I said. I don't know everything, but I do know that what I have been doing has not helped you, or me for that matter. Let's take a break and talk again tomorrow night. Take some time to think and reflect on what I have shared, then we can talk about what the new plan will look like, ok?

Jillian: Yeah— Whatever.

Setting: The following evening Mary shares her Navigation Plan with Jillian, She has 2 copies so that they can go through the plan together.

Mary: Jillian, I want this to be more of an agreement between us, than a dictation of rules. Even though I have made up my mind about certain things, I have a list of things I am willing to do to help you. I also have a list of things I will expect of you. I am willing to listen and work with you. But there will be boundaries and spelled out consequences that will follow if the limits are crossed.

What is expected of you:

Within two weeks you will have a full-time job.

You will begin paying rent— $100 per month, starting next month.

You are responsible for getting to work.

You will save $3000 over the next 12 months in a savings account.

Beginning today, I will have Zero Tolerance for:

Coming home drunk

Bringing drugs into our home

Talking to me with disrespect (cursing at me, yelling or screaming at me)

Your responsibilities around the house:

Trash Out to the street on Monday nights

Cleaning Bathrooms once a week

Making Dinner once a week

Cutting Grass every 2 weeks

Regular Clean Up after yourself

Communication and Interaction between us:

We will speak respectfully to each other.

We will communicate during a conflict with the common goal of peaceful resolution.

If you raise your voice, I will walk away until you are calm.

If you become volatile or threaten physical harm, you must leave, or I will call the police.

Goal: Your Independence: A-12 Month Plan:

You will get a place of your own and be entirely self-reliant 12 months from today.

This will give you enough time to save $3000 to move. The 12-month period is to provide you with the ability to save for your own place without the burden of other expenses. I will not check up on your savings commitment. You will have to move out, regardless of whether you have saved $3000.

What I WILL do to help you:

For the first two weeks of your new job, I will pay Uber for your transportation. You will pay me back when you get your first paycheck. Or, if you prefer, you can find other transportation.

If at any time over the next 12 months you demonstrate suspicious behavior, I will respectfully confront you. You cannot become defensive, but instead, understand my concerns and answer respectfully. If I feel it is warranted, I will ask you to take a drug test. Refusal will be considered positive for drug use, and you will have to leave immediately.

My goal is to help you become fully self-reliant. It is up to you to use the next 12 months to position yourself for independence. I have set a Move Out day of December 1, 2019. Whatever that takes will be up to you. It may mean that you find roommates to share expenses, or that you work three jobs to pay your bills. That's life. I love you and hope you make the best of my generous offer and use this opportunity to prepare to be on your own.

Do–Follow The Navigation Plan

Be prepared when your loved one has to face the consequences listed in your agreement. Make sure you are timely and consistent with addressing broken rules or crossed boundaries. Practice how you will respond

Script Possible Scenarios:

It is wise to role play your response for each boundary you have set. Role play your reactions to probable scenarios. Take the above example of Mary and her daughter Jillian, for instance. Mary should be prepared if a confrontation arises with Jillian. To prepare, Mary discusses her concerns with her shipmate, Jane. Jane is a dear friend who supports Mary and gives her honest feedback. Jane is also a source of accountability, which Mary needs to remain consistent. Mary recognizes the possibility that Jillian may test the boundaries by coming home drunk. In this hypothetical situation, Mary rehearses with Jane what her responses will be to Jillian. Jane plays the role of Jillian. They discuss what confronting her daughter might look like. They determine that it would not be wise to engage Jillian while she is drunk. It would likely not go well and could possibly get violent. So in this scenario, Mary waits until morning. The next morning Mary wakes her daughter before she leaves for work. Mary reminds Jillian of the zero tolerance house rule about drinking and that according to their agreement she has two choices. Mary encourages Jillian to re-enter treatment. She tells Jillian that if she goes directly to rehab, she will give her another chance to come home; once treatment is completed. Mary further tells Jillian that if she refuses to go, then she will have to leave the home that day. Mary also tells her daughter that if she decides to leave, that once she is settled at the new location, she can return to pick up the rest of her things. Jillian is hung over, yelling at her mother telling her to shut up and to stop overreacting. Mary remains calm and reminds her daughter the terms of their agreement and that she fully intends to follow through on what she has committed to do. Mary tells Jillian that she must be out of the home before Mary returns from work at 6:00 pm. If not then she will be forced to call the police to remove her.

Mary will have to do hard things but can be assured that she gave

Jillian the opportunity to help herself, Jillian choices make her alone responsible for what will happen next. This is why it is so important to have clear and spelled-out consequences in your agreement wording. The signed Navigation Plan Agreement stands as a witness that Jillian understands and agrees to honor her word. It also ensures what she can expect if she violates the agreement. Jillian's poor choice is what has landed her in the position of not having a place to live. Mary may not be able to predict what boundaries her daughter may cross, but she can be confident that she is prepared to respond wisely.

Confrontation is not something we generally enjoy, but, healthy relationships require it, and broken relationships will not heal without it.

It Takes Courage

Sherry finally had the courage to separate from her husband, John. For years he regularly came home drunk. One night his obnoxious and aggressive behavior escalated. The Police were called to their home by a concerned neighbor. When police arrived, the kids were hysterical, the husband was belligerent, and Sherry was crying uncontrollably. One of the children told the police that her Daddy pushed her Mommy. With that, John was hauled away in handcuffs. Days following the incident Sherry kept praying for the strength and courage to stand up to her husband and require change. She told John that she was not willing to put their children or herself through another night like that ever again. She asked him to stay with his brother for a time so that she could do some thinking. Expressing true remorse, her husband reluctantly agreed. Being away from his wife and kids was hard on John. He really loved his wife and adored their three daughters. As the couple discussed repairing the marriage, Sherry made a difficult decision. She told her husband that she loved him and wanted to save their marriage. Sherrie expressed that she really missed him and wanted him to come home, but with conditions. She told him that the only way she would stay in the marriage would be if he agreed to go to a drug and alcohol treatment center. At first, he flat out refused, stating that he did not have a problem. Weeks passed, and Sherry was lonely without her husband around, she often found herself with conflicting emotions. Many times she was very close to just dropping the whole thing and telling him to come home. But she was determined to stay the course. If John really wanted to save his marriage, then he had to choose; alcohol or his family. He chose his family and entered treatment.

John could have made a different choice. What if he decided to continue drinking? What if he decided to drive while intoxicated and died in a horrible car accident as a result? Then what?

Would that have made Sherry's boundary unloving or wrong? I don't believe so. This man had a wife willing to support his sobriety. She set limits because she loved him. Her motive for setting conditions was to save the relationship. We need to set boundaries that protect us while communicating love and support to the addicted people we love. We cannot allow ourselves to avoid doing so because we are afraid of what might happen if we do, but must follow through with the conditions we set in our agreements. At the same time, we also cannot let ourselves be tormented by guilt for someone else's terrible choices, which we have no control over. Remember, bad decisions that bring negative consequences or horrible outcomes are the sole responsibility of the person who made them.

Porthole: generally a circular window used on the hull of ships to admit light.

Troubled Waters

Addressing concerns is something we have a right to do, but delivery is everything.

It is common for someone in recovery to become defensive when confronted about a possible relapse. He will either be offended because he is sober and feels we are overreacting, or he will become defensive because he *is* using, to shame us for not trusting him. Our motive for confronting should be concern, not because we have made up our mind that the person is using. It is a good idea to remember that we are asking questions because it is the responsible thing to do. It is important to confront suspicions without accusing. Wording and posture can make all the difference.

1. If something seems off, it probably is.

2. If you suspect drugs in your house look for them. IT IS YOUR HOUSE!

3. Remember #1 and #2.

When you have a sense that something is not quite right, it probably isn't. If God reveals a problem, we must learn not to react, but to respond prayerfully. We should thank Him for shedding light and ask Him for discernment and direction on how to proceed. Listen for His wisdom. When we genuinely seek Him for help, He is faithful to answer. You may be scared, doubtful, and anxious but remember you have a plan. He will help you follow it through. Ask Him for strength to do the hard things. In executing the terms of your agreement, it will not always feel like you are demonstrating love. You have to remember that some of the hardest things you will do are the most loving things as well. When the boat rocks, troubled waters are most likely ahead. Be prepared to adjust the sails.

Take the Hall Family for example. When Ken's son began to spend more time in his room than usual, Ken took notice. He shared his concerns with his wife. They knew they needed to confront their son immediately. He had 6 months clean but slowly began isolating. This behavior was demonstrated during their son's active addiction, so it was understandable to suspect a possible relapse.

Scenario 1

Ken goes to his wife after observing a pattern of isolation by their son and says, "He's using again! I just know it! He's hiding in his room again!" Upon hearing this, his wife feels nauseous. She is fearful and angry. Together they storm into their sons' room already convinced he is using and demand that he take a drug test. Whether their son had relapsed or, not, this approach will no doubt lead to more conflict. If he's using, he will accuse them of not trusting him. If he's not using, he will accuse them of never believing in him. Conflict is guaranteed to follow.

Scenario 2

Ken takes notice that his son is spending more and more time in his bedroom. He checks his thoughts. Ken tells himself not to make assumptions and to believe that his son has not relapsed until it proves otherwise. He prays about how to handle his suspicions, then goes to his wife and shares his concern. He tells her that he believes for the best, but also wants to be wise and address what he has observed. His wife is grateful that her husband has not assumed the worst, and has included her in deciding the best way to confront their son. They agree to talk with their son when he returns home. Because they have a Navigation Plan, they already have a baseline on how to proceed.

They discuss this briefly and agree on how they will approach the situation–what they will say and how they will say it.

Let's look at an example of a planned response.

Ken: Tommy, your mother and I want to check in with you. We are not assuming anything or accusing you of anything. This is not to bring up the past, but instead to rely on it to help us ask the right questions.

Tommy: Ok, here we go again. What now? What's up? (a bit defensive)

Ken: "We have a responsibility based on history to come to you, Tommy. We ask you not to be defensive, but to help us understand Ok? We've noticed that you are starting to retreat to your room lately. As you know, that is a red flag for us, since isolating was present during your active addiction. So we want to ask you how you are doing. Are you struggling with anything? We want to help."

In the above scenario, Ken and his wife stick with the facts. When confronting their son, they are confident that they do not have to tiptoe for fear of offending their son with questions. Their demeanor and tone of voice demonstrate genuine concern. They understand they have a right to ask any question.(They were wise to point this out to Tommy when entering the family agreement with him). Tommy, on the other hand, must understand and accept that it is his past poor choices that have created the lens his parents are currently looking through. Tommy's parents are off to a good start in getting to the truth. Depending on how Tommy handles things as the conversation progresses will determine the next steps. Tommy could be agreeable and answer the questions to the satisfaction of his parents, or he could behave with more behaviors that indicate possible relapse. With the former, the family will have had a loving, and successful confrontation and trust can begin to reestablish. The later depends. If one or both parents allow their emotions to take over and start to get loud and begin making accusations, it can get very ugly–very quickly. However, if they remain calm while their son acts out, they will be in a position of quiet authority. Together they can make decisions following the exchange that demonstrate unity.

Ken and his wife already have an agreed-upon Navigation Plan in place. They have shared the plan of action with Tommy and his siblings. Tommy will have already initialed and signed a written Family Agreement, so he is well aware of the immediate consequences. His only question would be, will his parents really do what they have said they will do? If so, Tommy will experience the new way his parents deal with his addiction. He will be angry, but awakened that his parents are unified. Ken and his wife will begin to build trust with each other as well as the rest of the family. The Hall Family has a plan. They do not have to react but instead act according to plan. Of course, the whole purpose of a plan is to unify the family and bring peace to the home.

Remember when following the Navigation Plan the decisions you have previously made put your addicted loved one in the best position to choose sobriety— so take action with confidence. Based on the Hall's Navigation Plan, they have already **determined** what they would or would not allow in their home. They have already **decided** what would take place when certain situations present themselves. They have also committed to each other and the rest of the family to follow through and execute what they have promised to **do**.

Keep Your Word

They have also determined what would happen if their son failed or refused to submit to the test. They must now do what they said they would do and enforce the consequence–No Matter What.

It may feel like some of the suggestions in this book are impossible for you to do, especially if you are a people pleaser and conflict avoider. But remember, it helps no one if you let things continue as they are. If you change nothing, nothing changes. And isn't change what you want? It takes courage to go in a new direction, but at least you have a map this time! When it comes to maintaining focus and sailing steadily during this journey, nothing compares to having others to lean on for support. Many people I know find great comfort and gain renewed hope by attending Al-Anon Meetings. (meetings specific to family members or friends of someone battling Substance Use Disorder)

There is something unique about gathering with people who truly know what we are going through. It gives us validation and a sense of belonging. Assembling with people who are broken in the same places we are broken somehow helps us heal.

For anyone reluctant or unable to attend a meeting, there are many online groups and communities available. Of course, The Anchored Family Group is always a safe harbor to be authentic. It is a place to share feelings and struggles honestly— made up of people like you and me who are sailing the same sea. (hey, that's a rhythm)! It is a private, non-judgmental space with compassionate people offering encouragement and support. You might be saying to yourself, "That's great Des, but where is God? Where is He when I hurt so badly"? Well, I can tell you, it is not where you think.

> *Do not fear, for I am with you; do not be afraid, for I am your God. I will strengthen you; I will surely help you.*
>
> *Isaiah 46: 10*

FIVE

Where is God in the Storm?

"God hates me," she said with absolute certainty. My sister-in-law stared at me with angry, pain-filled eyes. Her statement felt like a dagger to my heart that pierced my soul–mostly because her words felt more true than any assuring promise or encouraging scripture. What was I to say to that? After all, her son had died of an accidental overdose. Not long after, her husband was airlifted to a Texas trauma unit when he was found unconscious and barely breathing on a dark highway. Man and motorcycle— mangled. She hopped on a plane to be at my brother's side. Just as she entered his hospital room in the ICU, her phone rang. It was a call from home; could things get any worse? Yes, they could and did. Her mother suffered a massive heart attack and died shortly after my sister-in-law boarded her plane to go be with my brother. If I had been her, I'd have felt like God hated me too. Actually, I have felt that way at times, or at the very least I have wondered if He even liked me.

A prayer taken from my journal March 2015,

> Lord, my circumstances feel more real to me right now than you. You say you love me, and I know it's true but what's happening in my family makes me feel like you just don't care. It hurts so much because I am asking you to meet me where I am, but I feel like you've abandoned me. I am trying to trust you, but it feels like things are getting worse, not better. I am angry, disappointed, and paralyzed by fear. I feel so alone Jesus. My faith is weak, and my heart is broken. Where are you?

The writer of Psalm 88 knows the feeling:

Lord, I cry out to you for help. In the morning I pray to you. Lord, why do you say no to me? Why do you turn your face away from me? I've been in pain ever since I was young. I've been close to death. You have made me suffer terrible things. I have lost all hope. Your great anger has swept over me. Your terrors have destroyed me. All day long they surround me like a flood. They have closed in all around me. You have taken my friends and neighbors away from me. Darkness is my closest friend.

What Anchor?

Often times we ask God to lead us beside still waters, but we find ourselves in a raging storm. For example, when we ask God to heal someone of cancer, and a scan shows three more lesions than the last. We feel ignored by Him, betrayed even. Is God listening? Does He really care? We ask ourselves, "If God is good why isn't He doing his job?" We all have unspoken expectations of God, don't we? We secretly accuse Him of not using His power the way we think He should. However, scripture is clear, God says that His ways are not our ways. There are many things we simply will not understand this side of heaven. At one point or another, I think we have all felt as if God has turned His back on us, or worse, is out to get us. But how we feel does not make something true. My favorite preacher, Dr. Tony Evans says, circumstances never measure God's love for us. He says this in his distinctive black Baptist, authoritative, you-better-get-this-voice:

> Our feelings should never dictate our trust in God. If we allow feelings and circumstances to determine our faith in God—we have bigger problems than we realize. Our faith would be tossed about never really sure of what to believe or who to trust. Scripture teaches that our faith must be in God who is faithful and true, despite what we are going through.

We need to continue going to God in prayer. The definition of insanity is doing the same thing and expecting a different result. Be insane when it comes to prayer. It's the only thing we can keep doing over and over again that offers the possibility of a different result.

One of my dearest friends, Donna, prayed for her addicted son for 15 years. She refused to allow her mind to run wild with "what if's." Her focus was on God. The day her prayers were answered she called me screaming with praise. Her son admitted himself to treatment. Soon after, so did her son's wife. Not long after, the sober couple established a home and regained custody of their five children. They now lead a thriving ministry that supports those seeking recovery. When we hear stories like this, they give us new hope for our own family members. But what if the story were different? What if her son stayed on drugs or succumb to his addiction? Does God now hate her? Would she abandon her faith, leave her church, and walk away from God? No-Donna is a true Proverbs 31 Woman. She has lived through enough trauma and heartache in her lifetime to know where her trust belongs. There is hope, but our hope must be in God not in the outcomes that we pray He will give us. Our loved ones have choices–and many hopes are shipwrecked when our prayers seem to go answered. The bottom line is this: God is responsible for what He does or does not do. By His own admission, God declares His sovereign rule over all things, and He makes no apologies about it. We have to decide whether we will trust Him when we don't understand. That is not to say we can't question Him. I think being honest with God about how we feel is necessary to a true relationship with Him. He doesn't have to tell us why He allows or causes anything, but He does have to keep his promise to help us get through the storm. Tony Evans says, "Faith is believing that God is telling the truth."

> *Do not fear, for I have redeemed you; I have called you by name, you are mine. When you pass through the waters, I will be with you; and through the rivers, they shall not overwhelm you; when you walk through fire you shall not be burned, and the flame shall not consume you. For I am the Lord your God, the Holy One of Israel, your Savior.*
>
> *Isaiah 43:1*

Walking on Water

Jesus told the disciples to get into their boat and cross over to the other side. They trusted His direction and found themselves in a dangerous storm. Sometimes obedience to God can lead to situations that cause us to wonder if God knows what He's doing. When Peter demonstrated faith by putting his foot outside the boat, his steps were sure. He walked on water with Jesus, for a little while anyway:

> *Immediately after this, Jesus insisted that his disciples get back into the boat and cross to the other side of the lake, while he sent the people home. After sending them home, he went up into the hills by himself to pray. Night fell while he was there alone. Meanwhile, the disciples were in trouble far away from land, for a strong wind had risen, and they were fighting heavy waves. About three o'clock in the morning Jesus came toward them, walking on water. When the disciples saw him walking on water, they were terrified. In their fear, they cried out, "It's a ghost!" But Jesus spoke to them at once. "Don't be afraid," he said. "Take courage. I am here!" Then Peter called to him, "Lord, if it's really you, tell me to come to you, walking on water." "Yes, come," Jesus said. So Peter went over the side of the boat and walked on water toward Jesus. But when he saw the strong wind and the waves, he was terrified and began to sink. "Save me, Lord!" he shouted. Jesus immediately reached out and grabbed him. "You have so little faith," Jesus said. "Why did you doubt me?" When they climbed back into the boat, the wind stopped. Then the disciples worshiped him. "You really are the Son of God!" they exclaimed.*
>
> *Matthew 14:22-33*

For the first few steps, Peter was able to walk, even as the storm raged around him. However, when he took his eyes off of Jesus and focused on the conditions, he began to sink. As he started to go under, Peter cried out to Jesus, who held Peter and led him to safety. As we trust God to guide us, we have to look to Him continually for courage and strength. We have to remind ourselves that He has the power to bring us through every storm to the other side. In the midst of it all, we have to remember that even the wind and the sea obey Him. Dr. Tony Evans reminds us that faith has to be active, "Faith is measured by feet, not by feelings. Faith is measured by walk, not talk. Faith is measured by life, not lips".

Watch Tony Evans in the link below to see why he is my favorite on YouTube.

Dr. Tony Evans: Trusting God in the Storm.
https://youtu.be/pFAxrpxjXuo

On the morning of April 16, 2014, in South Korea, a massive cargo ship set sail. It was not long into the journey that the ship turned on its side. Investigators reported that the vessel overturned because cargo shifted and forced the vessel off balance. Investigators found that at the time of departure, the ship was carrying 2,142.7 tons of cargo when its maximum allowance was 987 tons–causing the ship to sink. It can feel like the weight of the world is bearing down on us when we carry burdens we were never meant to carry.

Cargo Jesus?

Sometimes God speaks through unlikely people. I shouldn't be surprised really, after all, in the new testament, He spoke through a donkey. Why couldn't He communicate something profound through my biker brother? *Just kidding... but for real though...*

Not too long ago my brother Steve put words to what has been his struggle and mine, and perhaps yours. It was at our baby sister's funeral when he spoke to the sea of mourners facing her casket. He began by reading the well-known poem, "Footprints In The Sand":

Footprints

One night a man had a dream. He dreamed he was walking along the beach with the Lord. Across the sky flashed scenes from his life. For each scene, he noticed two sets of footprints in the sand; one belonged to him, and the other to the Lord.

When the last scene of his life flashed before him, he looked back at the footprints in the sand. He noticed that many times along the path of his life there was only one set of footprints. He also noticed that it happened at the very lowest and saddest times in his life.

This really bothered him, and he questioned the Lord about it. "Lord, you said that once I decided to follow you, you'd walk with me all the way. But I have noticed that during the most troublesome times in my life, there is only one set of footprints. I don't understand why when I needed you most you would leave me."

The Lord replied, "My precious, precious child, I love you and would never leave you. During your times of trial and

> suffering, when you see only one set of footprints, it was then that I carried you."
>
> – Unknown

My brother paused, wiped his eyes, and took a deep breath before speaking. He went on to say that the days leading up to the loss of our sister, broke him. He said that during that time, he was reminded of that old poem which caused him to reflect on his life and God's presence. While looking back, he painfully concluded that during the most trying times in his life, he never really felt carried by the Lord. Now, I can't say exactly how the conversation between him and God went for sure. But knowing my brother, God had some "splainin to do." As mourners quietly wept, my brother regained his composure and with tear-filled eyes continued to share. He said that while he was *calling God out* and demanding answers, God interrupted him–as if his honesty with God freed his heart and unchained God's voice: "The footprints in the sand are yours. Steve, I wanted to carry you, but you wouldn't let me; instead, you carried Me".

It was as shocking as it was profound. We all do this, don't we? We pour our hearts out, we plead for God to help us, then– *We carry*–Him. We take Him along with our burdens and carry them to where we hope to find rest for our weary souls. Under the weight of it all, we privately accuse God of abandonment. With each step, our feet sink deeper into the sand. I think when it really comes down to it, we all want a God we can carry, one we can control. Of course, we want God's will as long as it agrees with ours. Sure, we have faith in Him, as long as things turn out the way we believe they should.

In recent years, loss has stripped me of any facade or pretense. God says that His ways are not our ways. I have come to understand this to be very true. He has chosen to develop my character over the years in ways I would never have agreed to if He asked me. Who would willingly agree to suffer loss in order to become appreciative? Seriously— His ways for shaping and molding us into the image of Christ are never what we would expect. It's crazy to imagine or comprehend the mystery of how God refines our faith through suffering. I often wonder, would my compassion for bullied children be as deep, if I was not ruthlessly bullied by playground monsters? Or how much understanding would I have for someone with Major Depressive Disorder, if not for my own personal dark nights of the soul? Grief has enlarged my heart. Loss has gifted me with a greater appreciation for my family. Mistakes and poor decisions have taught me wisdom. It really can feel like we are walking alone during our most devastating trials in life. But what I have come to know is that during His perceived absence on the outside, God is doing important work on the inside. Heart Work, that He in His wisdom has determined cannot be achieved any other way. Life continues to teach me that deep faith only grows in desert places. In the garden, Jesus was deeply troubled knowing that His call to the cross was near. He agonized and asked God if there was another way to save us from our sin— There wasn't. When Jesus was dying on the cross, he cried out, "My God, My God, why have you forsaken me?" Jesus felt forsaken, but his darkest night dawned on the third day with a miracle that saved humanity. When our lives do not make sense, we have to trust God who promises to one day make sense of it all.

> *God's ways are as mysterious as the pathway of the wind and as the manner in which a human spirit is infused into the little body of a baby while it is yet in its mother's womb.*
>
> *Eccles 11:5 NIV*

When we encounter harsh elements, it is hard to think straight. Emotions rage and fears rise. Having a systematic plan in place can determine whether we sink or swim. We have to guard ourselves against threatening waves of discouragement. When we are faced for example, with news that a loved one has relapsed or gone missing, prayer is our safe-haven. It is in these times we have to cry out to God and remind ourselves that Jesus is as near as our own heart. Life is so unpredictable, and when we love someone in addiction or working recovery, it can be so intense. Personally, I have mapped a go-to response whenever I am faced with concerning circumstances or receive bad news of any kind. I go to God in prayer. I remind myself that He is my anchor. I rehearse the fact that The Almighty is not caught off guard by anything, and He will keep me steady when the sea rages around me. I remind myself that in every storm I face, God is at the helm.

Helm: a tiller or wheel and any associated equipment for steering a ship or boat.

SIX

Lifesavers, Loose Cannons, and Castaways

Lifesaver: a person who rescues another from the danger of death, especially from drowning. A person or thing that saves a person, as from a difficult situation or critical moment.
Grand-parents.[italicized emphasis mine]

Her pain filled eyes turned down—hardly able to look back up at me. Shameful tears broke the dam of stuffed emotions. She wished she could pull the words she had just spoken back into hiding, where no one would judge her. She looked around checking our privacy, hoping that no one heard her terrible secret. Her voice cracked in a whisper, "I love my grandchildren, it's just... I mean... I raised my kids, this is not how I imagined my life at 58 years old. I dreamed of being there in their lives, but not being solely responsible for them." As the words came from her mouth, her demeanor sank under the weight of her reality. "I'm sorry Des," she agonized with regret for expressing her true feelings. "It's just so hard." I handed her a tissue and nodded in understanding. I hugged her tight assuring her of my support. I find myself comforting many who are raising grandchildren these days. Parents of addicted adults have an incredible amount of daily grief. They are not only heartbroken and grieving because their adult child is sick, but they also have the added sorrow of watching their grandchildren suffer without parents. The daily responsibility of caring for small children (while trying to provide for them) can be overwhelming and exhausting. Jackie is raising her three grandchildren. Her daughter and son in law together are in active addiction living on the streets of Philadelphia. She battles depression and struggles most days to find the strength to put her feet on the floor. A loud crash coming from the kitchen gives her no choice. She leaps up like a Ninja and frantically follows the sounds of crying and yelling. Upon discovery, she sighs deeply in relief that no one is hurt. She scurries the kids out of the room as she grabs a broom to sweep up the glass, milk, and chocolate powder and wishes to herself that her worries could be mopped up as easily. And so it begins, another day of doing, caring, loving, crying and worrying. Her constant prayer is for her adult child to come to her senses, get help, and to be the parent her grandchildren need and deserve. She is baffled at how her daughter is able to trade these precious gifts to pursue what drugs will never give her. "What can I do?" She rhetorically asks herself, let the system raise them? Abandon them like their parents have? Who will protect them? Who will love them? Who will help them? —She will. She will—because she loves them more than life itself. Grandparents are remarkable people who are under-appreciated and deeply broken and some of the strongest people I have ever had the honor of knowing.

Loose Cannon: Someone that is off doing their own thing without regard to others. Believed to have its origin from the mayhem caused on ships when a cannon breaks free from its mooring during a storm or in battle.

"I can't stand junkies, hate them, I just can't stand the scumbags." He sat across from me at a barbecue when the conversation turned toward the nationwide heroin epidemic. My heart sank. My thought process came to a screeching halt, like a stopped record on a turntable mid-song. I stood frozen in shock that quickly melted into hot anger; I struggled to contain myself. I am not kidding when I say that it was only by God's power that I was able to restrain myself from literally karate chopping him in the throat.

As he continued his rant, I found myself using some humor to calm the rage inside me. I imagined my swift and targeted Kung Fu chop silencing him. In truth Thanks be to God for reminding me that, from the heart, issues flow. This man's heart and mind are filled with ignorance and pride. Have you been there before? I have. Thinking I know it all, speaking of what I think I know, instead of listening to understand. So what I decided to do was pray for him and encourage him to educate himself. In that moment, shutting him up might have felt really good, but, it would not change his heart—only God could do that. Next time I will be prepared. I will admonish him to do some soul-searching to determine why he feels the way he does. For shock value, I will also encourage him to explore why he thinks he is above others.

Judges and critics who have never been in the storm of addiction are ignorant to the countless variables that feed addictive behavior. A lack of education about the biological, emotional, environmental, and relational factors that attribute to the disease of addiction, breeds individuals like Barbecue Guy. Arrogant and pompous, they add to our pain with rude comments and hurtful statements. If you encounter someone like this, just pray. Don't argue, defend, or karate chop them. Try to remember that we were once where they are. Our desperation to help a loved one, pushed us to find answers. We made it our mission to educate ourselves about substance abuse, and it has helped us see with different eyes. Try to kindly educate those who just don't get it. Providing information helps people gain a broader perspective—resulting in deeper compassion toward people suffering in addiction. Scripture tells us that we should never hurt people with our words.

> *Slander no one, to be peaceable and considerate, and always to be gentle toward everyone.*
>
> *Titus 3:2*

> **Castaways:** a person who has managed to swim or float to a lonely island or shore after their boat has sunk.

I found this letter written by an unknown author on Facebook. It is powerfully humbling for any person who has ever taken a drink, smoked a joint, swallowed a pill, sniffed a line, tripped on acid or anything else considered harmless partying-back in the day:

> Hello, if you don't know I am an addict. I am one of the "junkies" you love to bash whenever someone mentions addiction on social media or hear it in conversation. I know it's hard to forgive the things we sometimes do because of our addiction, but I have a question for you. What is the worst thing you have ever done? Obviously, I won't get an answer to this question but think about it. The thing that you hate that you did. You know, that one thing that not too many people even know about. Well, what if everyone knew about it? What if for the rest of your life you were labeled by that one act that you would erase in a second if you had the chance? That is what being an addict is

like, kind of. Now, I don't feel like being an addict is the worst thing a person can be or do. You, however, feel like it's a terrible thing. Don't get me wrong: If I could erase it from my life, I would. In an instant, it would be gone, but I don't have that option. I can't even do what you do and pretend that this thing I did didn't happen. In order for me to ensure it never happens again, I have to work hard on making sure it doesn't. If I don't, my disease will tell me I can have a drink or do a line and not fall back into full-blown addiction, but I will. Do you work hard to make sure your worst thing never happens again? Yes, all addiction starts with a choice. The same damn choice you made when you were young and hanging out with friends. You drank the same beer I drank. The same pot I smoked. You even tried the same line of white stuff someone put in front of you at a party. You were able to walk away and not take it to the extreme....As children, we don't decide we would rather be an addict instead of a cop. You don't see children pretending that their dolls and stuffed animals are dope sick. When is the last time you talked to a little girl who told you she couldn't wait to grow up so she could turn tricks to feed the insatiable hunger of her drug addiction? My sister didn't tell me about her exciting plans to become homeless. My dad, not one time, told my mother to think twice before marrying him because he had high hopes of becoming an angry drunk. I damn sure didn't blow out my candles as a child wishing for a substance abuse disorder because I couldn't wait for the day my beautiful daughters were taken from me by CPS. I pray that you don't have to reevaluate these opinions because you find out your child or parent is an addict. If you do, just know that we will accept you into our community. We will help your loved one. Do you know why we would do that? Because we are good people who just want the chance to live like everyone else. *So please, before you write another post bashing people who are suffering, think about it. You not only hurt the people who have the disease, but you are also hurting everyone that loves them. You have people on your friend list or who might overhear you at work who have children who are suffering right this moment from addiction. What did they*

> *do to deserve the awful things you put out into the universe that do nothing but perpetuate hate and judgment? You have a right to your opinion. But no matter what, hurting people is wrong.*
> Author: Unknown [italicized emphasis mine]

> **Message in a Bottle:** a letter written on a scrap of paper, rolled-up and put in an empty bottle and set adrift on the ocean; traditionally, a method used by castaways to advertise their distress to the outside world

It has been said that we will never look into the eyes of someone God does not love. I believe that, and I think this letter is an important reminder that reckless words wound those He loves deeply— We do not have that right. We all need to examine our hearts and stop thinking we have the right to spew angry or judgmental words at anyone. At one point or another, we have all had a high opinion of ourselves. We observe other people and compare their moral failures to ours. Somehow, we determine that we are not that bad. It makes us feel better about ourselves. We use our standard to measure the outward actions of others and compare them to a pumped-up version of ourselves. But in reality, we have grieved God in the same ways— it's just not known by others. Most times, it is not even recognized by us.

> *Live in harmony with one another. Do not be proud, but be willing to associate with people of low position. Do not be conceited.*
>
> *Romans 12:16*

Judging another's battle is arrogant at best, and completely ignorant of God's grace, at worst. Jesus was angered by people who thought they were superior. He challenged their high mindedness and chastised those who believed themselves to be above others. Anyone who considers himself a Christian should be demonstrating Christ's love for His people. Jesus said that those who are sick need a physician. Scripture tells us to embrace the sick with God's love. If you are a member of a church, I encourage you to prayerfully consider talking with your pastor about addressing the National Opioid Epidemic. Drug addiction is not being spoken about from the pulpit. If you feel lead to speak with your pastor, check your motives and guard your delivery. Humility is what God honors. We all need to be reminded of our responsibility to demonstrate God's compassion and act according to His word. Caring for the addicted depicts what Jesus meant when he said, "I was sick, and you visited me." One church that has fully embraced struggling addicts and their families is the Calvary Chapel of Philadelphia. In an incredibly helpful booklet, "How To Minister to an Addict - A Guide For Pastors" [distributed by the church] the author says with great concern: "One huge need is for the problem of addiction to be spoken about from the pulpit in church."

Messages of acceptance and forgiveness breathe new hope into weary, broken people. True compassion and understanding demonstrated by God's people can turn a life around and transform a family. Many bedraggled, downcast, and suffering souls, are searching for God. Sadly, in some churches, they can't find Him.

God has been gracious to us and only when we truly understand that, are we able to extend grace to others. It is humbling when we consider that all we are, anything we have, and our very lives are gifts from God.

> *Once we, too, were foolish and disobedient; we were misled by others and became slaves to many evil pleasures and wicked desires. Our lives were full of resentment and envy. We hated others, and they hated us. But when the time came for the*

kindness and love of God our Savior to appear, then he saved us–not because we were good enough to be saved but because of his kindness and pity–by washing away our sins and giving us the new joy of the indwelling Holy Spirit, whom he poured out upon us with wonderful fullness–and all because of what Jesus Christ our Savior did so that he could declare us good in God's eyes–all because of his great kindness; and now we can share in the wealth of the eternal life he gives us, and we are eagerly looking forward to receiving it. These things I have told you are all true. Insist on them so that Christians will be careful to do good deeds all the time, for this is not only right, but it brings results.

Titus 3:3

There is no one answer to the problem of addiction. Many people have strong opinions on how to stop the epidemic, but personal passions can sometimes blind us to other valid avenues to consider. What works for one individual to maintain sobriety may not work for another. So many factors contribute to a person becoming addicted and finding addiction solutions is equally complex. We need to come together and listen to each other, respect opinions that are different from our own, and understand that we are all in the same boat. Anyone who loves a person that is imprisoned by addiction has the same crushed heart and raging battle within to keep hope alive–Every day. The same goes for how each family chooses to show love and support. What works for one family simply will not for another. We are all doing our best to figure out how to really help a loved one find freedom from addiction. Remember this when tempted to judge another's life and choices. There is only one judge, and it is not any of us.

SEVEN

Rescue Drowning Mates

Feed the hungry, and help those in trouble. Then your light will shine out from the darkness, and the darkness around you will be as bright as noon. The Lord will guide you continually, giving you water when you are dry and restoring your strength. You will be like a well-watered garden, like an ever-flowing spring.

Isaiah 58:10 NLT

Every time I attend an event, she's there. Whether it's to raise awareness, raise funds, or raise hope, Bonnie can be found. On the verge of a nervous breakdown, after her son was arrested for dealing, she reached out to leaders at a local church. The local prison ministry team members helped her through many difficult days. That was 10 years ago. Now, where the hell on earth dwells, Bonnie helps distraught family members fix their eyes on Heaven. She leads a weekly family support group and loves doing it.

I was a single parent and all alone. Since he was 14, my son was in and out of jail, treatment, recovery houses-he just didn't seem to want to get clean. It was truly heartbreaking. In 2014 after having so much trouble with depression, I was hospitalized for a short time. When I got out I contacted a leader of a local prison and recovery ministry in our town, The ministry team visited my son in jail. I attended recovery meetings and through the people I met there, God helped me and worked thru me. He made it clear to me that I was not alone in this roller coaster ride and even though I felt totally alone He was with me at all times. One day the Lord clearly spoke to me and told me that I could help the loved ones of people struggling with addiction. I thought to myself, "How could I possibly help them?" I still doubted myself and my abilities and thought I still had so much to learn. Today I advocate, educate and support those in addiction and their families. To me, it clearly feels like this is my one true calling. The fact that I had to get down to my own "rock bottom" only to discover that all I had to do was to stand on that rock and let Jesus pull me up and out has changed my life. I share my story with others to give them hope. I used to be so ashamed, I blamed myself for my son's addiction and for my daughter's problems. Now I'm meeting people who are exactly where I was with my kids 10 yrs ago. They don't know what to do, where to go or who to ask for help. I love being a part of the recovery ministry, and I love to witness to others about God's love for us and how He saved my life.

Bonnie is one of many amazing and selfless souls who allow God to redeem personal pain to resurrect hope for others. Carol Rostucher is another, in a recent article, a reporter puts a face to every mother with a child lost in addiction:

> Carol Rostucher knows all too well the pain of addiction. Her sister is a heroin addict and her 25-year-old son used to live on Kensington's streets after heroin took hold of his life. "My son said the first time he tried heroin he knew he was hooked,"

she said. "I don't know the feeling. I guess it's like euphoria." When her son was at the worst of his addiction, she patrolled Kensington – where she was born and raised — searching for him. With her son now in recovery and living out of state, Rostucher continues to patrol Kensington Avenue, playing the role of mom for many other young addicts, some of whom are looking to get clean and need guidance. While many people may have given up on these lost souls, including their own families, Rostucher refuses to do so. "Everyone thought my son was hopeless, everybody," she said. "I've have grown to love a lot of these people down here. I want to help them, I want to help them find their way out." Rostucher, who now lives in a nearby suburb, says she shows addicts in Kensington her son's photo from before he entered recovery. Many recognize him, she says, and they're shocked when she pulls out a photo of him after recovery wearing a button-up shirt with his face filled out and healthy. Then she tells them, "So if he can do it, why don't you think you can?" In February 2015, she created the group Angels in Motion to coordinate more volunteers to help people with addictions. "I worry for all of them," she said. "They deserve a second chance at life." Until something more is done about the growing heroin epidemic, she will continue to patrol the streets of Kensington. Before heading home, she made one last stop to see a man she knows is close to entering rehab. "I'm so proud of you," she said as she leaned toward the passenger window and handed him bottled water. ~Todd Reed America Tonight, contributing reporter Sarah Hoye,[sic]

Angels in Motion now has over 11,000 members who support and volunteer to help the suffering and downcast. This, to me, is what Jesus looks like among us.

His cousin John was just murdered. When he heard about the horrible way John died, He was overcome with sorrow. Even if He wanted to speak, He knew no words would come out. Surely, unanswered questions flooded his mind and rendered him speechless. No doubt, he needed time to process what just happened, so He withdrew from family and friends. He just wanted to be alone.

> *When Jesus heard about John, He left there privately in a boat and went to a secluded place. But when the crowds heard of this, they followed Him on foot from the cities. When He went ashore, He saw a large crowd, and felt profound compassion for them and healed their sick. When evening came, the disciples came to Him and said, "This is an isolated place and the hour is already late; send the crowds away so that they may go into the villages and buy food for themselves." But Jesus said to them, "They do not need to go away; you give them something to eat!" They replied, "We have nothing here except five loaves and two fish."He said, "Bring them here to Me."Then He ordered the crowds to sit down on the grass, and He took the five loaves and the two fish and, looking up toward heaven, He blessed and broke the loaves and gave them to the disciples, and the disciples gave them to the people, and they all ate and were satisfied. They picked up twelve full baskets of the leftover broken pieces. There were about 5,000 men who ate, besides women and children.*
>
> Matthew 14:13-19

With a broken heart full of sadness Jesus reached out to help others. He also gave us an example to follow when we are suffering. From a place of deep emotional pain, Jesus reached out to others in need. He healed the sick and fed the hungry. God will always help us as we help others, just as He promised:

> *He comforts us in all our troubles so that we can comfort others. When they are troubled, we will be able to give them the same comfort God has given us.*   2 Corinthians 1:4

What Wrecks You?

Bill Hybels gives a good description of people like Dana. In his book *Holy Discontent,* Bill says a wrecked person is broken so deeply about something that they must act. A wrecked person will stop at nothing to bring about change. They are people who make the pain that others experience–personal. It has been said that our deepest wounds position us to have the greatest impact. It is people like Dana Richie, who in the midst of private pain, asked one simple question, "How can I help?" I believe one of the most powerful ways God demonstrates His love is through wrecked people–Brave souls, willing to transform personal pain into public healing. Dana and her team roam city streets and provide basic human needs like food, clothing, and showers to those battling addiction. They also remind them that recovery is possible when they are ready. And when they are, the Never Give Up team is right there in their midst, ready for them! Hope is contagious. A personal mission can be life-saving for both the Hurting and the Wounded Healer. A description of the help provided by Dana's organization as described on the Never Give Up Facebook Page/Group:

> Mission and Purpose:
>
> We provide support, resources, and guidance for those who are homeless & struggling with addiction in the right direction when they are ready for treatment.
>
> We are a group of volunteers who have been touched by addiction on all different levels. Our main purpose is to lift the fallen, restore the broken, help heal the hurting and provide hope to the lost. We collect donations (clothes, shoes, snacks, candy, water, blankets, etc...) and take them out to the streets where there is a large number of homeless and addicted in Philadelphia & Bucks County. We offer an ear to listen and a heart for hope. We provide them with the resources available and help

guide those who are ready to treat. We do this out of love in our hearts. We are here to help people who often feel so hopeless find that hope again. We also have a women's shower night every Tuesday evening at 5:30 pm to 9:00PM. Offering showers to those women that are homeless and still in active addiction. We provide them with clothing, and most importantly toiletries. [sic]

What can one person do to help fix what's wrong in the world? Just ask Bonnie, Carol, or Dana.

> **High and Dry To be High and Dry:** A way of saying that something or someone is stranded without any hope of recovering the situation.

Many people struggling in addiction and those working recovery find it difficult to believe that they can have a powerful impact for good in this world. They think that their past disqualifies them to do great things. Nothing could be further from the truth. No one is beyond God's forgiveness or grace; anyone's history can be redeemed.

She lay on her bedroom floor, lifeless. After finishing up a three day drug binge, Michael Deleon went home to find his 63-year-old mother, dead. At first, it was believed that she died of natural causes, but an autopsy revealed that she had been strangled. At the time Michael was immersed in gang activity and closely connected to violent and dangerous people. On May 13, 1995, his mother, Catherine Theresa DeLeon became a target and victim by association. Michael's tangled gang ties cost his mother her life and cost him everything. Mother's Day is the most difficult day of every year for Mike since it was the events of that day over 20 years ago that changed everything. Deep regret and sorrow for his choices back then still sneak up and overwhelm him to this day, he told me:

> I believe that I am responsible for her death. I put her in that situation. I brought gang members into my life, into our house. I endangered her, and I am responsible for her death. I have to live with that every single day.

But he made another choice following the worst day of his life, a decision that today, brings hope and healing to countless parents. He's on a mission:

> My Mother's death is part of my story. The worst part, but still, only a part of my story. I did many bad things. I hurt many people. I broke nearly every law written, and I spent nearly 14 total years in prison and halfway houses for the crimes I committed and for ones that although I didn't commit, I am responsible for. I will never live a day where I don't have to live with this. That is why I will spend every day of my life trying to make a difference in the world.

Michael travels across the country to speak at schools to warn young people to never, ever get involved in gang-related activity. He speaks at churches and community events to educate and encourage broken-hearted families. Michael broadcasts inspiring true stories of individuals living successful recovery on his nationwide tour, Road to Recovery.

Although I have never met his mother, as a mother, I do know something about her. I know that she would have laid down her life willingly to those gang members if she knew it would save her son one day. I know she is looking down, proud. Mike and his wife Darla are two of the most amazing people I have had the privilege of knowing. Their work has saved thousands of young people from the prison of addiction. They should be feared by the drug cartel because if anyone could put drug dealers out of business, it's them.

We may not be able to travel the country with a message, but we can make a huge difference in our own family. God will help us we just have to let Him. Often God brings hope and healing to us as we help others. When Nehemiah observed that his comrades were growing weary and distraught because of the deadly threats of the enemy, he reminded them of what was at stake. He strengthened himself in the Lord and implored them to stand firm:

> *When I saw their fear, I stood and said to the nobles and officials and the rest of the people: "Do not be afraid of the enemy; [confidently] remember the Lord who is great and awesome, and [with courage from Him] fight for your brothers, your sons, your daughters, your wives, and for your homes."*
>
> *Nehemiah 4:14*

Captain James Lawerence said, "Don't give up the ship!" "Tell them to fire faster; don't give up the ship!"

I will never give up the ship, and I pray that you never do either. With God all things are possible.

NEVER GIVE UP THE SHIP!

PART II

NEVER GIVE UP THE SHIP!

He will anchor my soul
I will praise Him
in the storm

Bon Voyage

ONE

All Hands on Deck

Gathering our family members together is a good place to begin sailing in a new direction. In your own words tell your family that you are aware of how bad things are within the family. Also, acknowledge your contribution to the situation. Express your desire to make things better by changing course and then ask your loved ones to join you on your voyage. It is idealistic to think that all family members will be willing to join you. Quite honestly they are exhausted and many times fed up with the way addiction has hijacked their lives by association. Many family members become relationally distant and resentful. This is because for so long the focus of the family has been on the person struggling with drug use. Resistance is certainly understandable. It is important to explain that you recognize that the entire family is being impacted negatively. You can offer hope by communicating that their participation will benefit everyone. Even if no one gets on board, it is critical that you make a plan and set sail.

It is crucial that you surround yourself with what I call "strong Shipmates." These are individuals or groups you can rely on if you are doubting yourself, feeling discouraged, or need support when sailing gets rocky. You can never have too much support. Surrounding yourself with strong, confident, and trustworthy people is always wise. So even if you have to set sail without your immediate family, it's important to join your Anchored Family Support Group on Facebook to help you stay on course. Your reluctant family members may reconsider, once they observe the positive impact the Navigation Plan is having on you.

Determine Weather Conditions

Does my help, really help?

Ask yourself, could I actually be helping someone to remain irresponsible and immature? Is it possible that what I believe to be helping, is actually hindering someone's growth?

The following questions have blanks to fill in the name of the loved one that you have tried to help. Write the person's name on the line for each question that applies to you. Please actually write the person's name on the blank line for each question. Some of the questions are designed to help identify the common denominators in family conflicts. This process will uncover the true state of how your family functions from day to day. It will also help to determine what changes are necessary to best position your loved one to choose sobriety. Answering these questions will help you gain insight and clarity about unhealthy patterns. It will also give you the confidence needed to execute changes that will benefit your entire family.

Ask Yourself:

1. Have I loaned _____ money repeatedly, and seldom (if ever) been repaid?

2. Have I paid for education and/or job training for _____ in more than one field?

3. Have I finished a job or project that _____ failed to complete because it was easier than arguing?

4. Have I paid bills that should have been paid by _____?

5. Have I avoided talking about negative issues because I feared _____ response?

6. Have I bailed _____ out of jail or paid for his legal fees?

7. Have I given _____ "one more chance" and then another and another?

8. Have I ever returned home at lunchtime (or called) and found _____ still in bed sleeping?

9. Have I wondered how _____ gets money to buy cigarettes, video games, new clothes, and such but can't afford to pay his own bills?

10. Have I ever "called in sick" for _____ lying about her symptoms to her boss?

11. Have I threatened to throw _____ out and didn't?

12. Have I begun to feel that I have reached the end of my rope because of the chaos _____ brings into my life?

13. Have I begun to hate both myself and _____ for the state in which I live?

14. Am I constantly worried because the financial burden _____ addiction is exceeding on my monthly family budget?

15. Have I noticed growing resentment in other family members because of _____ behavior and actions?

16. Have I noticed that others are uncomfortable around me when issues arise that involve _____?

17. Have I noticed an increase in profanity, violence, and/or other unacceptable behaviors demonstrated by other family members because of the frustration of _____ addiction?

18. Have I ignored obvious signs that _____ is taking items from my home, including money, valuables, and other personal property?

Now go back and identify any behaviors or actions you are bound to repeat unless you plan otherwise.

Write them in the space provided.

For example:

- It doesn't help when I give money to _____ because when I support him financially, he is not motivated to work.

- It is not helpful to pay _____ fines, because it doesn't motivate her to stop incurring them.

- It is not helping when I do not allow _____ to experience reality. When I cushion consequences for his behavior and actions, it only impedes his ability to function in the real world.

TWO

Decide— Course Change

What will Change

What changes can I make that may actually help?

Put a check mark next to the things you will do that will require the dependent person to think for themselves. What will you do to position a dependent person to make immediate changes?

__ Stop the money flow

__ Stop paying fines

__ Stop paying credit card bills

__ Stop making excuses

__ Stop managing messes

__ Stop walking on eggshells to avoid conflict

__ Stop allowing lazy or unproductive behavior

___ Stop taking excessive calls for advice on every little decision they face

___ Stop answering questions that require me to think of solutions to their problems constantly

Add any actions you will take that are not listed above:

1. _____
2. _____
3. _____
4. _____
5. _____

Based on your selections, think through and write the likely reaction you may get from the dependent person. (note: this will help you prepare to enforce consequences)

Think through your selections above. Be sure you are willing to allow natural consequences to play out without interfering before including them in your Navigation Plan.

For Example:

> If you stop the money flow, the dependent person will not have money. They will have to get a job.
>
> If you stop paying fines, they will have to set up a payment plan with the courts or risk being picked up for an outstanding warrant. It is their choice.

If you stop thinking for them, they will have to think through situations and come up solutions. They will have to manage the results of any decisions they have made.

1. _____

2. _____

3. _____

4. _____

5. _____

Place a check next to any personal patterns you want to break to allow growth and foster independence

I will also:

___ Stop taking control of situations.

___ Stop trying to control people.

___ Stop trying to control outcomes.

___ Stop making emotional decisions

It Has Been Said, When We Stop They Start

THREE

Do–Follow The Map

New Direction

The pages in this section contain templates to map your course. Choose the appropriate template that applies. The templates are relationship specific and are organized as follows:

- Spouse
- Adult Child
- Dependent under 18 Years of age

Each title will include:

- Your Personal Navigation Map Template to determine your new route. (this is for your personal use to **prepare** you to present the Navigation Plan to your loved one).

- A Navigation Plan Template detailing the new course to **present and share** with your loved one and a Navigation Plan Agreement

Template. (This two-page document will be presented to your loved one to read and sign.)

Of course, you can write in this book. However, I recommend getting a one half inch binder to keep your Navigation Map and Navigation Plan to make it easy to add information or make changes. You can print all templates and the Tackle Box and resources pages to keep together in your binder as your go to guide. Bound by Love Anchored in Truth printable worksheets can be found at **DesireeArney.com** at no cost. Just use the code "Anchor" for access. Or you may also order the accompanying Bound By Love—Anchored In Truth Workbook.

Navigation Map and Navigation Plan Templates for Spouse

This section is for your personal mapping. It's purpose is to prepare you to fill out the Navigation Plan to present to your spouse.

**Use this template to map your new journey. Fill in the blanks to determine your direction and how you will navigate troubled waters. Once completed, you will then fill in your Navigation Plan details and present it to your spouse.

Navigation Map Template for Spouse

Prepare for the Conversation You will have with Your Spouse.

Pre-Conversation: Casually mention your desire to make changes. What will you say?

⚓ Write a loose script below:

_____

_____

_____

_____

_____

_____

_____

_____

_____

_____

Prior to the sit-down meeting with your spouse mention your desire to do things differently. The goal of this conversation is to set a time and place to discuss your overall concerns. Include the fact that you have already made some decisions that will impact him, which you will share during the upcoming meeting.

⚓ Write what you will likely say:

The Day of the actual sit-down meeting to introduce the Navigation Plan to your spouse:

Open the conversation by explaining your genuine concerns about your marriage and family. Be clear in communicating that you are not willing to allow things to remain the same. Assure your spouse of your commitment to the marriage.

⚓ Write a few specific examples that you will share with them to make your point. (ex: I am afraid if we do not get counseling, that we will grow further apart). Use "I" statements.

_____
_____
_____
_____
_____
_____
_____
_____
_____

Express your desire to have a healthy marriage. Highlight the fact that your decisions are designed to help change the things that threaten your relationship.

⚓ Write a loose script of what you might say (ex: I want to support your sobriety, but we have to have a plan, I want to heal as a couple and leave the past behind–so some things have to change)

Detailed Change of Course

⚓ List the things you have decided to stop doing immediately: (ex: calling her out of work for illegitimate reasons, working to smooth over fractured relationships for her).

Write your answers below:

⚓ List behaviors or actions for which you will have Zero Tolerance (ex: bringing drugs into the home, violence toward you or the children, using drugs)

_____
_____
_____
_____
_____
_____

What will happen?

Example:

    If this occurs: You bring drugs home.
    This will happen: You will have to find another place to live.

If this occurs	This will happen
1. _____	1. _____
2. _____	2. _____
3. _____	3. _____
4. _____	4. _____
5. _____	5. _____

⚓ List things you will not accept any more (ex: excuses, blaming others, cursing, yelling, or screaming at you)

_____
_____
_____
_____
_____
_____

What will happen?

Example:

    If this occurs: You begin yelling at me.
    This will happen: I will walk away until you stop.

If this occurs	This will happen
1. _____	1. _____
2. _____	2. _____
3. _____	3. _____
4. _____	4. _____
5. _____	5. _____

⚓ List your expectations for Spousal and Parental responsibility (ex: financial obligations, maintaining the family budget)

What will happen?

Example:

    If this occurs: You do not work to contribute to our bills
    This will happen: I will move to an affordable place without you.

If this occurs	This will happen
1. _____	1. _____
2. _____	2. _____
3. _____	3. _____
4. _____	4. _____
5. _____	5. _____

⚓ List relational expectations to rebuild trust (ex: willingly submit to a random drug test, full disclosure regarding plans or activities when asked)

_____
_____
_____
_____
_____
_____

What will happen?

Example:

> If this occurs: If you refuse a drug test
> This will happen-I will assume you are using drugs, I will file for separation.

If this occurs	This will happen
1. _____	1. _____
2. _____	2. _____
3. _____	3. _____
4. _____	4. _____
5. _____	5. _____

⚓ List obligations and expectations with details (ex: work together to take care of the physical, emotional, and spiritual needs of the children or sharing school responsibilities like attending soccer games and conferences)

⚓ List the things you are willing to do to help your spouse be successful at working their recovery and reaching personal goals (ex: attend sober events with them, restrict other family members from bringing alcohol into the home, join the gym with them)

_____

_____

_____

_____

_____

_____

_____

The Template on the next page is your Navigation Plan to share with your spouse. Print 2 copies to go over at your planned discussion time. To agree to terms, your spouse will initial where indicated and then you will both sign the agreement. If your spouse is not agreeable, then you have some difficult decisions to make.

AGREEMENT

Navigation Plan

This agreement is intended to support your recovery and to rebuild trust in our marriage. My prayer is that having this contract will foster healing in our relationship. I hope that together we can build a strong and unified family.

Detailed Change of Course

⚓ Things I will stop doing immediately:

_____

_____

_____

_____

_____

_____

initial _____

⚓ Behaviors or Actions that I will have for Zero Tolerance

_____
_____
_____
_____
_____
_____

initial _____

What will happen?

	If this occurs		This will happen
1.	_____	1.	_____
2.	_____	2.	_____
3.	_____	3.	_____
4.	_____	4.	_____
5.	_____	5.	_____

initial _____

⚓ Things I will not accept any more.

_____
_____
_____
_____
_____
_____
_____

initial _____

What will happen?

If this occurs	This will happen
1. _____	1. _____
2. _____	2. _____
3. _____	3. _____
4. _____	4. _____
5. _____	5. _____

initial _____

⚓ Responsibilities around the house:

_____
_____
_____
_____
_____
_____

initial _____

What will happen?

If this occurs	This will happen
1. _____	1. _____
2. _____	2. _____
3. _____	3. _____
4. _____	4. _____
5. _____	5. _____

initial _____

⚓ To begin rebuilding trust I expect you to:

initial _____

What will happen?

If this occurs	This will happen
1. _____	1. _____
2. _____	2. _____
3. _____	3. _____
4. _____	4. _____
5. _____	5. _____

initial _____

⚓ Obligations and expectations with specific details:

_____
_____
_____
_____
_____
_____

initial _____

What will happen?

If this occurs	This will happen
1. _____	1. _____
2. _____	2. _____
3. _____	3. _____
4. _____	4. _____
5. _____	5. _____

initial _____

⚓ The amount of time I expect you to take action or specific dates I expect execution of the terms in this agreement:

initial _____

⚓ Things I am willing to do to support your sobriety:

initial _____

Navigation Plan Signatures

I have initialed where indicated to acknowledge that I understand the terms in this Navigation Plan. Having read the terms, I commit to honor the terms. I understand that all parties involved are expected to honor this agreement.

My signature on this indicates my commitment to the terms of this agreement. I understand that if I do not honor the expectations listed in this agreement, it will result in the appropriate action. I must abide by this agreement.

Print Name _____

Signature _____

Date _____

Print Name _____

Signature _____

Date _____

Navigation Map and Navigation Plan Templates for Adult Child

This section is for your personal mapping. It's purpose is to prepare you to fill out the Navigation Plan to present to your adult child.

**Use this template to map your new journey. Fill in the blanks to determine your direction and how you will navigate troubled waters. Once completed, you will then fill in your Navigation Plan details and present it to your adult child.

Navigation Map Adult Child

Prepare for the conversation you will have with your Adult Child.

Pre-Conversation: Casually mention your interest in making some changes. What will you say?

⚓ Write a loose script below:

_____
_____
_____
_____
_____
_____
_____
_____
_____

Prior to your actual sit down meeting with your adult child mention your desire to do things differently. The goal of this conversation is to set a time and place to discuss your overall concerns. Include the fact that you have already made some decisions that will impact them, which you will share during the upcoming meeting.

⚓ Write what you will likely say:

Prepare for **The Day** of the actual sit-down meeting to introduce the Navigation Plan to your adult child.

Open the conversation by sharing your new knowledge about how your intended help is hindering their growth.

⚓ Write a few specific examples that you will share with them to make your point. (ex: Paying their bill-teaches irresponsibility)

_____
_____
_____
_____
_____
_____
_____
_____
_____

Explain your new position on how you intend to help them in the future. Highlight the fact that the help you will offer is intended to position them for change and independence.

⚓ Write a loose script of what you might say (ex: I want to support your sobriety, or I want to encourage you to become self-sufficient and fully independent).

Detailed Change of Course

⚓ List the things you have decided to stop doing immediately: (ex: Buying them cigarettes or calling them out of work).

Write your answers below:

⚓ List behaviors or actions for which you will have Zero Tolerance for (ex: Bringing drugs into your home, drunk driving, not working).

_____
_____
_____
_____
_____
_____

What will happen?

Example:

    If this occurs: If you bring drugs into our home

    This will happen: You have to leave immediately.

If this occurs	This will happen
1. _____	1. _____
2. _____	2. _____
3. _____	3. _____
4. _____	4. _____
5. _____	5. _____

⚓ List things you will not accept anymore at all (ex: excuses, blaming others, cursing, yelling, or screaming at you)

_____

_____

_____

_____

_____

What will happen?

Example:

> If this occurs: If you start to blame others
> This will happen: I will walk away until you take ownership.

If this occurs	This will happen
1. _____	1. _____
2. _____	2. _____
3. _____	3. _____
4. _____	4. _____
5. _____	5. _____

⚓ List your expectations for shared household responsibilities (ex: Take trash to the street on Tuesday or cut the grass every 2 weeks or as needed).

_____
_____
_____
_____
_____
_____

What will happen?

Example:

If this occurs: If you do not cut the grass
This will happen: I will pay a lawn service and charge you.

If this occurs	This will happen
1. _____	1. _____
2. _____	2. _____
3. _____	3. _____
4. _____	4. _____
5. _____	5. _____

⚓ List relational expectations to rebuild trust (ex: submit to a random drug test, provide full disclosure regarding plans or activities when asked).

_____
_____
_____
_____
_____
_____

What will happen?

Example:

    If this occurs: If you refuse a drug test
    This will happen: You have to move out

If this occurs	**This will happen**
1. _____	1. _____
2. _____	2. _____
3. _____	3. _____
4. _____	4. _____
5. _____	5. _____

⚓ List obligations and expectations with details (ex: secure a job within 2 weeks, begin paying $50 per week rent starting 30 days from now, work 40 hours a week).

_____
_____
_____
_____
_____
_____

What will happen?

Example:

If this occurs: If you do not work 40 hours weekly.
This will happens: I will not allow you to stay.

If this occurs	This will happen
1. _____	1. _____
2. _____	2. _____
3. _____	3. _____
4. _____	4. _____
5. _____	5. _____

Set Timeline with Dates to Execute Transitions

⚓ List the expected transitions and the amount of time or specific date for each (ex: Begin applications for obtaining an apartment in May, a month before moving out date or begin packing 2 months before moving out date).

_____
_____
_____
_____
_____
_____

How are you willing to help your adult child gain independence?

⚓ List the things you are willing to do to help your adult child succeed in reaching goals (ex: Assisting them to make a list of action items to accomplish what it takes to move out, but not do it for them).

_____
_____
_____
_____
_____
_____

The Template on the next page is your Navigation Plan that what you will share with your adult child. Print 2 copies to go over at your planned discussion time. To agree to terms, your Adult Child will initial where indicated and then you will both sign the agreement. If your Adult Child is not agreeable, then you have some difficult decisions to make.

Navigation Plan Agreement

This agreement is intended to support your recovery and provide you with opportunities for growth and independence. I/we are utilizing this tool to rebuild trust. My/Our prayer is that having this contract will foster healthy relationships within our family My/We hope that our family will become strong and unified

Detailed Change of Course

⚓ Things I will stop doing immediately:

_____

_____

_____

_____

_____

_____

initial _____

⚓ Behaviors or Actions that I will have for Zero Tolerance for

_____
_____
_____
_____
_____
_____

initial _____

What will happen?

If this occurs	This will happen
1. _____	1. _____
2. _____	2. _____
3. _____	3. _____
4. _____	4. _____
5. _____	5. _____

initial _____

⚓ Things I will not accept any more.

_____
_____
_____
_____
_____
_____
_____

initial _____

What will happen?

If this occurs	This will happen
1. _____	1. _____
2. _____	2. _____
3. _____	3. _____
4. _____	4. _____
5. _____	5. _____

initial _____

⚓ Responsibilities around the house:

_____
_____
_____
_____
_____
_____

initial _____

What will happen?

If this occurs	This will happen
1. _____	1. _____
2. _____	2. _____
3. _____	3. _____
4. _____	4. _____
5. _____	5. _____

initial _____

⚓ To begin rebuilding trust I expect you to:

_____

_____

_____

_____

_____

_____

_____

initial _____

What will happen?

If this occurs	This will happen
1. _____	1. _____
2. _____	2. _____
3. _____	3. _____
4. _____	4. _____
5. _____	5. _____

initial _____

⚓ Obligations and expectations with specific details:

_____
_____
_____
_____
_____
_____
_____

initial _____

What will happen?

If this occurs	This will happen
1. _____	1. _____
2. _____	2. _____
3. _____	3. _____
4. _____	4. _____
5. _____	5. _____

initial _____

⚓ The amount of time I expect you to take action or specific dates I expect execution of the terms in this agreement:

_____

_____

_____

_____

_____

_____

initial _____

How I am willing to help you gain independence?

⚓ Things I am willing to do to assist you in gaining independence:

_____

_____

_____

_____

_____

_____

initial _____

I have initialed where indicated to acknowledge I have read and understood the terms in this agreement. Having read the terms, I commit to comply and honor the terms. I understand all parties involved are expected to honor this agreement.

Navigation Plan Agreement Signatures

My signature on this indicates my commitment to honor the terms of this agreement. I understand if I do not meet certain expectation listed it will result in the appropriate action. I will abide by this contract.

Print Name _____

Signature _____

Date _____

Print Name _____

Signature _____

Date _____

Print Name _____

Signature _____

Date _____

Navigation Map and
Navigation Plan Templates
for
Child Under 18

This section is for your personal mapping. It's purpose is to prepare you to fill out the Navigation Plan to present to your child.

**Use this template to map your new journey. Fill in the blanks to determine your direction and how you will navigate troubled waters. Once completed, you will be ready to introduce your Navigation Plan to your child.

Navigation Map for Child Under 18 Living in Your Home

Pre-Conversation: Causally mention your interest in making some changes. What will you say?

⚓ Write a loose script below:

_____
_____
_____
_____
_____
_____
_____
_____

Prior to the sit-down meeting with your child mention your desire to do things differently. The goal of this conversation is to set a time and place to discuss your overall concerns. Include the fact that you have already made some decisions that will impact them, which you will share during the upcoming meeting.

⚓ Write what you will likely say:

Prepare **The Day** of introducing the Plan to Your Child

Open the conversation by explaining your new knowledge about how your well-intended help is hindering their growth.

⚓ Write a few specific examples that you will share with them to make your point. (ex: paying their car payment-teaches irresponsibility)

_____
_____
_____
_____
_____
_____
_____
_____
_____

Express your new position about how you intend to help them in the future. Highlight the fact that your decisions are designed to help position them for change.

⚓ Write a loose script of what you might say (ex: I want to support your sobriety, or I want to encourage you to do and be your best)

_____
_____
_____
_____
_____
_____
_____
_____

Detailed Change of Course

⚓ List the things you have decided to stop doing immediately: (ex: paying for fuel or buying them cigarettes)
Write your answers below:

⚓ List behaviors or actions for which you will have Zero Tolerance for (ex: bringing drugs into your home, drunk driving, not working)

_____
_____
_____
_____
_____
_____

What will happen?

Example:

    If this occurs - If you bring drugs into our home
    This will happen - I will call the police to handle it.

If this occurs	**This will happen**
1. _____	1. _____
2. _____	2. _____
3. _____	3. _____
4. _____	4. _____
5. _____	5. _____

⚓ List things you will not accept anymore at all (ex: excuses, blaming others, cursing, yelling, or screaming at you)

_____

_____

_____

_____

_____

_____

What will happen?

Example:

    If this occurs: If you start to blame others

    This will happen: I will walk away until you take ownership

If this occurs	This will happen
1. _____	1. _____
2. _____	2. _____
3. _____	3. _____
4. _____	4. _____
5. _____	5. _____

⚓ List your expectations for shared household responsibilities (ex: take trash to the street on Tuesday or cut the grass every 2 weeks or as needed)

_____
_____
_____
_____
_____
_____

What will happen?

Example:

    If this occurs: If you do not cut the grass
    This will happen: I will pay a lawn service and charge you.

If this occurs	This will happen
1. _____	1. _____
2. _____	2. _____
3. _____	3. _____
4. _____	4. _____
5. _____	5. _____

⚓ List relational expectations to rebuild trust (ex: submit to a random drug test, provide full disclosure regarding plans or activities when asked)

_____
_____
_____
_____
_____

What will happen?

Example:

    If this occurs: If you refuse a drug test

    This will happen: I will involve the school guidance counselor to mandate treatment

If this occurs	This will happen
1. _____	1. _____
2. _____	2. _____
3. _____	3. _____
4. _____	4. _____
5. _____	5. _____

⚓ List obligations and expectations with details (ex: secure a part time job within 2 weeks, begin paying 20 per month toward cell phone bill starting 30 days from now)

_____
_____
_____
_____
_____
_____

What will happen?

If this occurs: If you do not work at least 15 hours weekly.
This will happen: I will shut off your cell phone

If this occurs	This will happen
1. _____	1. _____
2. _____	2. _____
3. _____	3. _____
4. _____	4. _____
5. _____	5. _____

⚓ List the expected transitions and the amount of time or specific date for each (ex: begin filling out applications for jobs on Monday, the payment start date for cell phone).

How are you willing to help your child gain more independence?

⚓ List the things you are willing to do to help your adult child succeed in reaching goals (ex: assist them in making a list of action items to accomplish, discuss how to write a resume, but not do it for them)

The Template on the next page is your Navigation Plan that you will share with your child. Print 2 copies to go over at your planned discussion time. To agree to terms, your child will initial where indicated and then you will both sign the contract. If your child is not agreeable, then you have some difficult decisions to make.

Navigation Plan Agreement

This agreement is intended to support your recovery and provide you with opportunities for growth and independence. I/we are utilizing this tool to rebuild trust. My/Our prayer is that having this contract will foster healthy relationships within our family My/We hope that our family will become strong and unified

Detailed Change of Course

⚓Things I will stop doing immediately:

_____

_____

_____

_____

_____

_____

_____

initial _____

⚓ Behaviors or Actions that I will have for Zero Tolerance for

_____

_____

_____

_____

_____

_____

initial _____

What will happen?

If this occurs	This will happen
1. _____	1. _____
2. _____	2. _____
3. _____	3. _____
4. _____	4. _____
5. _____	5. _____

initial _____

⚓ Things I will not accept any more.

_____
_____
_____
_____
_____
_____

initial _____

What will happen?

If this occurs	This will happen
1. _____	1. _____
2. _____	2. _____
3. _____	3. _____
4. _____	4. _____
5. _____	5. _____

initial _____

⚓ Responsibilities around the house:

_____
_____
_____
_____
_____
_____

initial _____

What will happen?

If this occurs	This will happen
1. _____	1. _____
2. _____	2. _____
3. _____	3. _____
4. _____	4. _____
5. _____	5. _____

initial _____

⚓ To begin rebuilding trust I expect you to:

_____
_____
_____
_____
_____
_____
_____

initial _____

What will happen?

If this occurs	This will happen
1. _____	1. _____
2. _____	2. _____
3. _____	3. _____
4. _____	4. _____
5. _____	5. _____

initial _____

⚓ Obligations and expectations with specific details:

_____

_____

_____

_____

_____

_____

initial _____

What will happen?

If this occurs	This will happen
1. _____	1. _____
2. _____	2. _____
3. _____	3. _____
4. _____	4. _____
5. _____	5. _____

initial _____

⚓ The amount of time I expect you to take action or specific dates I expect execution of the terms in this agreement:

initial _____

⚓ How I am willing to help you gain independence?
Things I am willing to do to assist you in gaining independence:

initial _____

I have initialed where indicated to acknowledge I have read and understood the terms in this agreement. Having read the terms, I commit to comply and honor the terms. I understand all parties involved are expected to honor this agreement.

Navigation Plan Agreement Signatures

My signature on this indicates my commitment to honor the terms of this agreement. I understand if I do not meet certain expectation listed it will result in the appropriate action. I must abide by this agreement.

Print Name _____

Signature _____

Date _____

Print Name _____

Signature _____

Date _____

Print Name _____

Signature _____

Date _____

There is nothing easy about any of this. There will be days when you feel defeated. There will be times when you feel weak and need guidance. Hook into hope by having systems in place to rely on when you are struggling. Your support network is critical in getting through difficult situations. List people, groups, and verses that encourage and strengthen you. Write a prayer for your loved one. Use the Relational Response Template to record how you react to certain situations. This tool can help identify patterns of response you may want to change. Changing the way you interact with a loved one in addiction can have very positive results.

My sincere prayer is that this book will encourage and strengthen you during this difficult time. I pray that your decisions position your loved one to make different choices for a better life. You are brave. You can love a person in addiction by making changes in yourself that may lead them out. God is with you. With Him all things are possible.

Desirée Arney

Certified Family Recovery Specialist

FOUR

Tackle Box

Hook into Hope

Remember these things:

- God is with you.

- God will help you.

- You are not alone.

- Your prayers are heard by God.

- God sees your tears.

- God understands your pain.

- God will comfort you if you ask Him.

- You have choices.

- Your feelings are valid.

- You can heal.

- You will get through this storm.
- God will help you.

And these things:

- "No" is a complete sentence.
- When you need support call one of your Shipmates.
- When you need reinforcement–send out an SOS.
- Read verses that give you strength out loud.
- Join the Anchored FaceBook Group.

Enlist three trusted, supportive, and sound-minded shipmates as personal anchors. These should be individuals who have read your Navigation Map and understand the direction you have chosen to take on this journey. Shipmates should be people who will hold you accountable to follow the map when fear threatens your resolve to stay the course. These should be people on call ready to remind you of God's promises to rehearse faithfulness with you.

My Shipmates:

1. _____
2. _____
3. _____

> **SOS:** an international code signal of extreme distress, used especially by ships at sea. An urgent appeal for help. Signals to call for reinforcements.

When an unexpected life threatening storm rolls in, send out an SOS. Call on your Rescue Operations Crew for reinforcements. Rescue members are people who are willing to find resources to help you and who will pray with you and for you. Family support group members can make great crew members because most are experienced sailors with a boatload of resource contacts to assist you.

My Rescue Crew:

1. _____

2. _____

3. _____

4. _____

5. _____

FIVE

Private Quarters

Pray–Pray– Pray

Prayer is simply talking to God and listening for his voice. Prayer is a conversation between you and God that should be as easy as talking to your most trusted friend. Bring your family member to God in prayer daily. You may want to write out a prayer to have ready in times that are especially challenging because sometimes we don't even know what to pray for. Scripture says that the Holy Spirit prays for us when we struggle in prayer.

> *And in the same way–by our faith–the Holy Spirit helps us with our daily problems and in our praying. For we don't even know what we should pray for nor how to pray as we should, but the Holy Spirit prays for us with such feeling that it cannot be expressed in words. And the Father who knows all hearts knows, of course, what the Spirit is saying as he pleads for us in harmony with God's own will.*
>
> *Romans 8:26-27 Living Bible (TLB)*

My Prayer

_____

Date _____

Print several copies for your Navigation Map Binder

My Journal

Date _____

Print several copies for your Navigation Map Binder

My Scripture Verses

Date _____

Print several copies for your Navigation Map Binder

Emotional Response Worksheet

Date _____

Situation

Thoughts

Feelings

Your Response

Print several copies and add to your Navigation Binder

SIX

Captains Orders

Trust Him

God calls us to trust Him in the storms of life. Rehearse and remember His Word. When He seems distant or silent, it is often God calling us to come closer to him. Keep praying.

> *You faithfully answer our prayers with awesome deeds, O God our savior. You are the hope of everyone on earth, even those who sail on distant seas. Trust in him at all times, you people; pour out your hearts to him, for God is our refuge. Psalm 62:8 TLB*

> *My eyes are red from crying, my stomach is in knots, and I feel sick all over. My people are being wiped out, and children lie helpless in the streets of the city. Lamentations 2:11 CEV*

> *Hear my cry, O God; listen to my prayer. From the ends of the earth, I call to you, I call as my heart grows faint; lead*

me to the rock that is higher than I. For you have been my refuge, a strong tower against the foe. Psalm 61 NIV

Let your hearts be turned to me, so that you may have salvation, all the ends of the earth: for I am God, and there is no other. Isaiah 45:22 BEB

Fear not, for I have redeemed you; I have called you by name, you are mine. When you pass through the waters, I will be with you; and through the rivers, they shall not overwhelm you; when you walk through fire you shall not be burned, and the flame shall not consume you. Isaiah 43:1-2 ESV

And He is before all things, and in Him, all things hold together. He will hold you together. He will keep you. Jesus loves you. He is not punishing you. He is not pleased by watching you suffer. When you suffer He suffers. He will keep you. He will pull you through. He won't allow you to fall apart. Colossians 1:17 ESV

But this I call to mind, and therefore I have hope: The steadfast love of the Lord never ceases; his mercies never come to an end; they are new every morning; great is your faithfulness. "The Lord is my portion," says my soul, "therefore I will hope in him." Lamentations 3:21-24 ESV

O Lord God, I cried out; O great and awesome God who keeps his promises and is so loving and kind to those who love and obey him! Hear my prayer! Nehemiah 1:5 BEB.

Print a copy to add to your Navigation Binder

God's Invitation

If you are unsure about who God is, ask Him. Ask Him to reveal Himself to you and lead you as you pray. God promises to listen to your prayers. He waits for you.

Read the following verse and ask God to show you what it mean for you.

> For this is how God loved the world: He gave his one and only Son, so that everyone who believes in him will not perish but have eternal life.
>
> John 3:16 NLT
>
> My Anchor God–My Hope God's Word
>
> *When a man takes an oath, he is calling upon someone greater than himself to force him to do what he has promised or to punish him if he later refuses to do it; the oath ends all argument about it. God also bound himself with an oath, so that those he promised to help would be perfectly sure and never need to wonder whether he might change his plans. He has given us both his promise and his oath, two things we can completely count on, for it is impossible for God to tell a lie. Now all those who flee to him to save them can take new courage when they hear such assurances from God; now they can know without a doubt that he will give them the salvation he has promised them. This certain hope of being saved is a strong and trustworthy anchor for our souls, connecting us with God himself behind the sacred curtains of heaven, where Christ has gone ahead to plead for us from his position as our High Priest. Hebrews 6:16*

I waited patiently for the Lord; he turned to me and heard my cry. Psalm 40:1

May the God of hope fill you with all joy and peace as you trust in him, so that you may overflow with hope by the power of the Holy Spirit

Romans 15:13

Print a copy to add to your Navigation Binder

Additional reading and helps:

The Co-dependent is a spirit divided from itself — Russell Gillette

Co-Dependency

We may become so consumed with our addicted loved one that we develop an addiction of our own. We can become addicted to a person.

Common characteristics of co-dependency

- Feeling overly responsible for the feelings and behaviors of others
- Constant need for approval from others
- Difficulty making decisions
- General feelings of powerlessness over one's life
- A basic sense of shame and low self-esteem over perceived failures in their life

Misconceptions about Co-dependency

Many co-dependent people appear to be very self-sufficient, "Strong" and in control of their lives.

Example: "Everyone thinks I am so strong, and all of my friends and relatives come to me with their problems, but if they only knew the real me they would be very surprised. Sometimes it's all I can do just to get through each day."

Co-dependency Today

Current research in Family Systems is revealing that co-dependency is a condition that can emerge from any family system where certain unwritten, even unspoken, rules exist.

The Co-dependent:

- Learns to do only those things which will get him/her the approval and acceptance of others
- Denies much of who he or she really is, with loss of self-identity and self-awareness
- Sees the needs of others as more important than the needs of themselves

Enabling

In an Addictive Family System, the word Enabler defines the behaviors of the Co-dependent.

- The Enabler is an individual who reacts to the symptoms of the illness (disease of addiction)
- The Enabler shields the dependent person from experiencing the full impact of the harmful consequences of the Addiction.
- The higher the enabling, the greater the fusion of those individuals.

Correlation between the Enabler and the Chemically Dependent.

1. How the Disease affects the Co-Dependent
2. How the Disease affects the Enabler

Excuses behavior of the chemically dependent
Self-worth becomes tied to the Dependent person (Fusion)
Growing feelings of guilt, embarrassment, and anger

Progression of Enabling

1. Stage One – Protection. Small tasks are done for the dependent such as calling in sick, getting them out of jail, paying for attorney fees.

2. Stage Two – Controlling. Larger responsibilities are taken over such as the handling of financial matters, supplying room and board for a young adult, or trying to control the dependent's chemical use.

3. Stage Three – Super People or Martyr. Begins to receive increasing positive feedback for "hanging in there" or "going the extra mile," At this stage, the enabler has grown so accustomed to their role that new found sobriety for the chemical dependent creates a traumatic emotional upheaval.

Why People Enable

1. Deluded about the situation - Not aware of their enabling

2. Feelings of apathy, tiredness, and inadequacy - Keep them from trying new approaches to the problem

3. Feelings of Fear – Scared for the dependent and feel a need to protect the helpless and themselves.

4. They get good feelings for being responsible - Being in control gives them a position of power.

5. Keeps them from looking at their own issues.

Common Characteristics

1. That co-dependent's are controlling because they believe that others are incapable of taking care of themselves.

2. That they typically have low self-esteem and a tendency to deny their own feelings.

3. They are excessively compliant, compromising their own values and integrity to avoid rejection or anger.

4. They often react in an oversensitive manner as they are often hyper-vigilant to disruption, troubles, or disappointments.

5. They remain loyal to people who do nothing to deserve their loyalty.

Victim Mentality

- Many who suffer substance Use Disorder adopt into Victim Mentalities.

- Victim symptoms include but are not limited too:

- Blaming – "My mother, my father, my spouse, my siblings, the police did such and such to me. "It isn't my fault. I can't help it".

- Negativity – The glass is always half-empty. Objectivity is lost to distortions that support a negative interpretation.

- Poor Me – Stories are skewed by the victim to create sympathy. "Poor me, poor me; pour me another drink."

- Drama – The victim makes others' problems his or her own.

Victim symptoms include but are not limited to:

- Needy-People, frequently and unconsciously, precede the victim's name with "poor." Poor old Johnny he never _____.

- Seeks help – again, again and again. The victim searches for a rescuer; someone who will magically fix him or her.

- Sickness – Illnesses are exacerbated and exaggerated as an often successful means escaping responsibility and attracting the longed for attention, pity and care-taking.

Being a Victim is not just a diagnosis, it is a way of life.

Moving from Codependency to Interdependency

- Person must rise above family emotionality and develop a loyalty to self that is not dominated by covert loyalties to previous generations.

- Must gain a clear, clean title to our own destiny, unencumbered by debts or events of the past.

The Long Road out of Co-dependency and into Recovery

New found sobriety can stress (chronic anxiety) the family by disrupting patterns of interacting until new roles are generated. The new person in recovery begins practicing new behaviors which throw the family into chaos when their behaviors, that have been the norm in dealing with the Addictive person, no longer work.

Family responses to a Newly Recovering person:

- A family member can replace the addicted person's role by becoming the family's Alcoholic/Addict. This immediately resolves the crisis, as family members can maintain their old roles and live by the old rules.

- The family may dissolve into many parts. The other parent may divorce the recovering parent.

- The family might have had so much pain recently, that they are willing to go to great lengths to get some relief. Meaning that the family may reach out for support and recovery as a unit.

- The family may undertake the deep work and commitment that is required to develop a whole new set of family rules.

What is Detachment?

- Detachment – is neither kind nor unkind. It does not imply judgment or condemnation of the person or situation from which we are detaching. Separating ourselves from the adverse effects of another person's Alcoholism/Addiction can be a means of detaching: this does not necessarily require physical separation. Detachment can help us look at our situations realistically and objectively.

- Detachment – Allows us to let go of our obsession with another's behavior and begin to lead happier and more manageable lives, lives with dignity and rights, lives guided by a Power greater than ourselves. We can still love the person without liking the behavior.

Traits of a Healthy Family

The Healthy Family:

- Communicates and listens.
- Affirms & supports one another.
- Teaches respect for others.
- Develops a sense of trust.
- Has a sense of play and humor.
- Exhibits a sense of shared responsibility.
- Teaches a sense of right and wrong.
- Has a strong sense of family in which rituals and tradition abound.
- Has a balance of interaction among members.
- Has a shared spirituality core.
- Respects the privacy of one another.
- Shares leisure and meal time.
- Admits to and seeks help for problems.

**adopted and modified from Dolores Curran's, *Traits of a Healthy Family*.

Dana Cohen explains codependency:

> Codependency means addiction to a person or a relationship. A codependent person works so hard to control and fix someone else. That his/her own life is in turmoil as a result. Because no one can really control anyone else, the others' troubles are mostly due to patterns only they can change; a codependent person is in for one painful disappointment after another.

How to Change Enabling Behaviors

When we begin to identify and change our behaviors, they don't just disappear all at once. Recovering and changing takes time and practice, lots of practice.

Do not:

- Make excuses or lie to others.
- Continue useless arguments.
- Clean up their messes.
- Pay bills you're not responsible for in areas that do not affect your basic health or well-being.
- Make threats you're not 100% willing to follow through on
- Play detective follow them around to meetings destroy your property searching for evidence.
- Make their doctors appointments for them.
- Do their laundry.

Do:

- Create a safe environment.

- Provide positive reinforcement and offer encouraging feedback.

- Remind them why they stop using and what they are like prior to using.

- Develop a contract together.

- Attend a 12 step meeting with or without them.

- Allow them to know how you're feeling .

- Encourage him to be honest with others about their addiction.

- Realize that you do not have to be a 24 seven on-call support system for them.

- Approach them if you suspect relapse.

- Have boundaries, set them, verbalize them, and follow through on them.

Effective Communication:

- Always uses "I" statements: I think, I feel, I hear, avoid demanding words: should, must have.

- Be mindful of nonverbal communication body language and facial expressions.

Dana Cohen MA, M.Ed 1018

Considerations for Parents of an Addicted Child

- Your actions and parenting are not what caused your child to become an addict.

- Perhaps there are many things that you would do differently if you had them to do over. But keep in mind at the time you made what you thought were the right decisions.

- Don't waste your energy and affect your own health by going over and over the past and endlessly second-guessing yourself the path to recovery, until they had hit their own personal rock bottom and are ready to recover.

- What you believe your child's rock bottom to be and what they believe it to be can be very different. You may think that one trip to the hospital due to an overdose will surely turn them around. For your child, it may take even more severe consequences.

- Saying to your child "If you love me you would get clean and sober" will never work. It's not that they don't love you; it's that they are addicted.

- Don't for a moment believe that your child who does love you, is not capable of lying and stealing when in active addiction.

- Bailing your child out of trouble caused by their addiction is not protecting them. It is enabling them to continue their addiction without consequences. Facing the consequences for their addictive behavior early may swiftly motivate change.

- Bailing your child out of jail if they should be arrested is not always the right thing to do. They will have time to reflect on their choices. Jail is also a place many do not want to return. Jail is a natural teacher.

- Telling your child, you love them unconditionally is always right. Telling them, you don't like and won't condone or support your behavior when they're actively using is also right.

- Your child can be more manipulative and cunning in their drug-seeking behavior than you would ever imagine. It is okay and appropriate to tell your child that they cannot use your car, have money, or jeopardize your home.

- You may reach a point where you need to tell your child that they are not allowed to be in your home. Protect yourself, your family, your health, finances, and assets

- Loving your child isn't always enough.

- Your addicted child will cause himself more pain than you can imagine and all the love you have for them can't prevent or stop it.

- They may lose friendships, relationships with family members and be alienated from everyone in the family. They may lose everything they have because of their drug use, you still love them even when they're at their worst.

- The guilt and shame they feel may cause them to doubt your love, and they may push you away.

- Always let them know that you believe that they can recover.

- Trust God with your life and your child's life, whatever each day brings God promises to be with you.

Resources:

SMART Recovery

SMART Recovery is an abstinence-based, not-for-profit organization with a sensible self-help program for people having problems with drinking and using. It includes many ideas and techniques to help you change your life from one that is self-destructive and unhappy to one that is constructive and satisfying. SMART Recovery is not a spin-off of Alcoholics Anonymous. No one will label you an "alcoholic," an "addict" or "diseased" nor "powerless," and if you do not believe in a religion or spirituality, that's fine, too. We teach common sense self-help procedures designed to empower you to abstain and to develop a more positive lifestyle. When you succeed at following our approach, you may graduate from the program, or you may stay around to help others. SmartRecovery website 2018

Use this link to learn more: https://www.smartrecovery.org.

Al-Anon for families impacted by addiction:
    Alcoholic Spouse / Partner
https://al-anon.org/newcomers/how-can-i-help-my/alcoholic-spouse-or-partner/
    Alcoholic Child
https://al-anon.org/newcomers/how-can-i-help-my/alcoholic-child/
    Alcoholic Parent
https://al-anon.org/newcomers/how-can-i-help-my/alcoholic-parent/
    Alcoholic Sibling
https://al-anon.org/newcomers/how-can-i-help-my/alcoholic-sibling/
    Grandchild in an Alcoholic Home
https://al-anon.org/newcomers/how-can-i-help-my/grandchildren-living-with-an-alcoholic/
    Alcoholic Friend
https://al-anon.org/newcomers/how-can-i-help-my/alcoholic-friend/

There is no magic formula that enables you to help someone stop–or cut back– on his or her drinking. Alcoholism is a complex problem, with many related issues. But Al-Anon can help you learn how to cope with the challenges of someone else's drinking. It may be that you could help matters by changing some of your own behaviors that make things worse. It may be possible for you to find a healthier way to respond to these challenges. Again, there are no easy answers. But Al-Anon meetings offer the opportunity to learn from the experiences of others who have faced similar problems. While simple problems may have simple solutions, the solution to complex problems is more difficult to explain. Al-Anon simplifies a complex problem by suggesting a "One Day at a Time" approach, which takes things one step at a time.

At every Al-Anon meeting, you can hear people explain how Al-Anon worked for them. That may be the best place to start to learn about Al-Anon–One Day at a Time. Al-Anon members come to understand problem drinking as a family illness that affects everyone in the family. By listening to Al-Anon members speak at Al-Anon meetings, you can hear how they came to understand their own role in this family illness. This insight put them in a better position to play a positive role in the family's future. Some research shows that when problem drinkers enter a recovery program, their chances for success are improved when they are supported by family members who are in a family recovery program such as Al-Anon. Al-Anon website 2018

Use this link to learn more or to find a meeting near you: *https://al-anon.org*.

Nar-Anon Family Groups

The Nar-Anon Family Groups is primarily for those who know or have known a feeling of desperation concerning the addiction problem of someone very near to you. We have traveled that unhappy road too, and found the answer with serenity and peace of mind. When you come into the family group, you are no longer alone, but among true friends who understand your problem as few others could. We respect your confidence and anonymity as we know you will respect ours. We hope to give you the assurance that no situation is too difficult and no unhappiness is too great to be overcome. Nar-Anon website 2018

Use this link to learn more or to find a meeting in your area: **https://www.nar-anon.org**

Facebook Online Support Groups:

    The Spiritual Addicts Mom

    The Addicts Mom

    Recovery is Possible

Sober Housing and Addiction Treatment

    phoenixrecoveryhouse.com

    kingdomhouserecovery.com

    http://www.silverliningsrecoverycenter.com

    https://genesishouse.net

    truelightrecovery.org

    http://www.poconomountainrecoverycenter.com

Organizations:

Parent-To-Parent Coalition, in the spirit of unity, offers strength and hope in support for families and their children suffering the ravaging effects of drug and alcohol addiction. http://parent2parentnj.org 2018

Steered Straight, reaches youth and young adults through motivational speaking, life-sharing seminars, and interactive curriculum. We Provide youth with real-life examples of negative consequences that resulted from making poor decisions. Impact the minds of youth to steer their lives in positive ways, and encourage them to make positive life choices. Give kids the ability to develop a sense of understanding about the positive and negative choices in their lives. Reduce the number of young people who end up in the criminal justice system due to making poor decisions. http://www.steeredstraight.org 2018

Conquering Life Prison and Recovery Ministries, CLPRM PO Box 1624 Southampton, PA 18966 http://CLPRM.orgCLPRM.org

Beacon Of Hope Bucks Co. Our mission is to educate, motivate, and celebrate those on their journey of recovery by identifying and removing obstacles/barriers that stand in their path. Find them on facebook @ Beacon of Hope Bucks Co.

Notes:

The Emotionally Destructive Marriage: How to Find Your Voice and Reclaim Your Hope by Leslie Vernick Published by Watermark Press 12265 Oracle Boulevard, Suite 200 Colorado Springs, Colorado 80921 copyright 2013

Setting Boundaries with Your Adult Children copyright © 2008 by Allison Gappa Bottke Published by Harvest House Publishers Eugene, Oregon 97408 www.harvesthousepublishers.com.

***Total Transformation* by James Lehman https://www.empoweringparents.com Copyright 2004 Audio.

Enabling Check List 2017 Nancy Shaul, Published by Will Books 2017. Used by permission

***From "Problem Child" to Child Behavioral Therapist:* James Lehman's Personal Transformation By Elisabeth Wilkins

***Footprints in the Sand*, Author Unknown, Boardofwisdom.com, 2019. 12 individual authors lay claim to this poem. 17 US. Code § 107, Fair Use 2018

Scripture quotations marked BBE are taken from the *Basic English Bible*, 1949/1964 Bible in Basic English, Public Domain printed in 1965 by Cambridge Press in England. Published without any copyright notice.

Scripture quotations marked (NIV) are taken from the *Holy Bible, New International Version®*, NIV®. Copyright © 1973, 1978, 1984, 2011 by Biblica, Inc.™ Used by permission of Zondervan. All rights reserved worldwide. The "NIV" and "New International Version" are trademarks registered in the United States Patent and Trademark Office by Biblica, Inc.™

Scripture quotations marked (AMP) are taken from the *Amplified Bible*, Copyright © 1954, 1958, 1962, 1964, 1965, 1987 by The Lockman Foundation. Used by permission.

Scripture quotations marked (TLB) are taken from *The Living Bible* copyright © 1971. Used by permission of Tyndale House Publishers, Inc., Carol Stream, Illinois 60188. All rights reserved.

Scripture quotations are taken from *The Message*, copyright © 1993, 1994, 1995, 1996, 2000, 2001, 2002 by Eugene H. Peterson. Used by permission of NavPress. All rights reserved. Represented by Tyndale House Publishers, Inc.

Scripture taken from *the Contemporary English Version,* copyright: American Bible Society 1991, 1992, 1995; Anglicizations British and Foreign Bible Society 1996, Used by permission

How to Change Enabling Behaviors, 2018 Dana Cohen M.A, M.Ed Used by permission 2018.

Alcoholic/Addict Family By Russell Gillette, LPC, LADC public domain 2019

Breaking Free of the Co-Dependency Trap. Barry K. Weinhold, Ph.D. & Janae B. Weinhold, Ph.D. 2008

**Beyond Codependency*, by Melody Beattie, 1989

**Family Evaluation* by Michael E. Kerr and Murray Bowen, 1988

**Family Therapy in Clinical Practice* by Murray Bowen, M.D. 1988

**Self-Pity Booklet* by Gil Baker 2016

**The Therapeutic Genius of Pia Mellody,* by John Bradshaw, MA (article was taken from website addictionrecoveryreality.com. 2013

Alcohol and Other Drug Treatment Initiative, Level II Training Manual, Sacramento Co., DHHS, Robert S. Caulk, Director, public domain

Substance Abuse Treatment and Family Therapy, A Treatment Improvement Protocol, Tip #39, US DHHS. public domain 2016

**Unless otherwise noted, definitions are taken from http://dictionary.comdictionary.com, 2018

Urbandictionary.com 2019 fair use

**Pirates http://glossary.comglossary.com 2018

Health Network, Chemical Dependency Program, Presenter; Mavonn Ellis, PH.D.

Cedar Vale ATU Out-Patient Office, Family Treatment Program handbook, public domain 2018

**I'll Quit Tomorrow*, by Vernon E. Johnson 1973

**The Co-dependence; Misunderstood* ---Mistreated by Anne Wilson Schaef, 2013

**indicates material in accordance with Fair Use, http://www.law.cornell.edu/uscode/17/107.shtml Title 17 U.S.C. Section 107.2018

Recommended Reading:

Dreamseller, An Addiction Memoir by Brandon Novak and Joe Frantz. If you can handle the language, this book will help anyone who does not struggle with addiction to see with different eyes. It is so well written that I actually felt like I was there watching the events in real time as they played out.

Personal favorites:

    Shattered Dreams by Larry Crabb

    The Shack by William Paul Young

    Your Secret Name by Kary Oberbrunner

ABOUT THE AUTHOR

Certified Biblical Counselor, Desiree has a passion for helping people embrace their individual worth & divine calling. Author of the children's storybook collection *Once Upon a Tea Pot* and teaching as The Tea Lady, she was a Princess with a Purpose for nearly 13 years. She taught etiquette and Character Education at a host of schools both public and private brewing up magic for young hearts from Children's Museums to Barnes & Noble and everywhere in between. Desiree wears many hats. Desiree speaks on many topics, but the message is always the same–Jesus. Now a Family Recovery Specialist, she is active in helping families impacted by addiction by facilitating Anchored Support Groups using material taken from her book.

Desiree offers leadership training several times a year for those wishing to start a Bound by Love Anchored in Truth support group in their church or community.

For more information, or Keynote inquires please visit:

DesireeArney.com

Pennsylvania Certification Board Certified Family Recovery Specialist

Made in the USA
Middletown, DE
28 February 2022

61958240R00113